6840403536 1 154

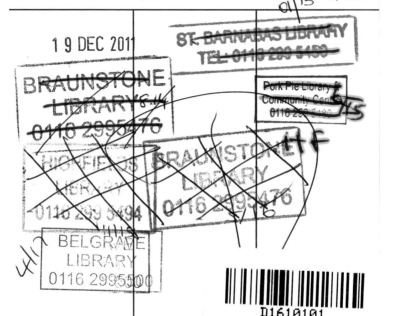
Book due for return by last date shown.
if not reserved by another user it may be renewed.

24/7 - Renewals, Reservations, Catalogue
www.leicester.gov.uk/libraries
Charges may be payable on overdue items

ROTA

The Last
Edwardian
JESTER
MR HARRY DALE AND
HIS MUSICAL FAMILY

Colin Dale

First published in 2010 by
Colin Dale
32 Greenbank Gardens
Edinburgh
EH10 5SN

ISBN: 978-0-9566024-0-4

British Library Cataloguing-in-Publication Data
A catalogue record for this book is available
from the British Library.

Design: Mark Blackadder

Printed and bound in the UK by the MPG Books Group,
Bodmin and King's Lynn

CONTENTS

INTRODUCTION AND ACKNOWLEDGEMENTS

I am aware that writing a biographical family history is nothing new in these days of expanding genealogical research. However, I think this particular story about a branch of the Dale family is a little unusual as it concerns the entertainment profession in the Victorian and Edwardian periods when major social changes were taking place throughout Britain. The transformation from an essentially agricultural economy to an industrial one had started before Victoria was crowned queen in 1837 and the movement of people into the urban environment accelerated after her coronation, creating a market for a whole spectrum of new services and activities. Amongst these, the demand for entertainment found its roots in the music hall and the circus, and many performers from all walks of life entered the profession seeking fame and fortune. My ancestors, starting with Henry Thomas Dale, were amongst them, and whilst none of them were leading stars, they made a reasonable living and had some success, so their various stories seemed worth telling. There is much written material on the well-known stars and household names of the Victorian and Edwardian periods but little has been published about the lesser folk of the music hall and the circus; I hope the pages that follow address this omission.

Bringing together this book has involved a number of people who have helped, guided and encouraged me over a period of several years. My journey of research started with Edinburgh genealogist Ian Stewart, who showed me the basics and stimulated my interest, and I was then encouraged to put pen to paper by local historian Malcolm Cant, Nicola Wood read the script, while designer Mark Blackadder brought it all together. I am very grateful to these individuals.

Details, photographs and other assistance have come from family members throughout the UK, in particular Alan Dale, Harry Dale, Keith Dale, Rina Dale, Rita Dale, Kevin Howarth and others. I thank them all for their patience and assistance. I also pay tribute to the unsung heroes of several family history societies especially the Manchester & Lancashire FHS the Powys FHS, and the Scottish Genealogy Society who have solved problems for me, and to library staff throughout the country who have responded to my queries, provided information and have been positive in their attitude towards me. The information in the book has been obtained from these and many other sources and, as a consequence, discrepancies and errors may have occurred, so that complete accuracy cannot be guaranteed, and any mistakes are mine alone.

I cannot know what any of the people featured within this book would have said about the contents, but I am hopeful they might have discovered some snippet of information that was new to them.

Colin Dale
Edinburgh, 2010

THE FAMILY OF MR HARRY DALE

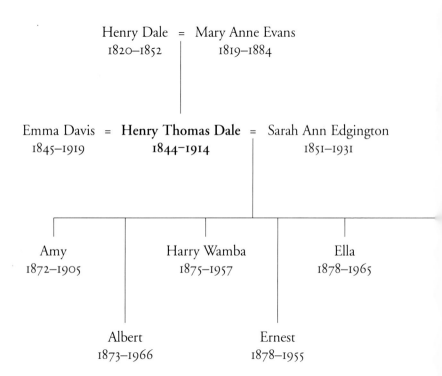

Henry Dale = Mary Anne Evans
1820–1852   1819–1884

Emma Davis = **Henry Thomas Dale** = Sarah Ann Edgington
1845–1919   **1844–1914**   1851–1931

Amy
1872–1905

Harry Wamba
1875–1957

Ella
1878–1965

Albert
1873–1966

Ernest
1878–1955

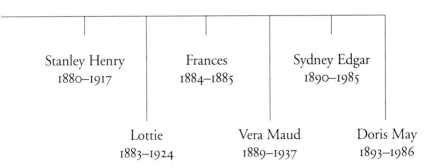

Stanley Henry
1880–1917

Frances
1884–1885

Sydney Edgar
1890–1985

Lottie
1883–1924

Vera Maud
1889–1937

Doris May
1893–1986

THE DAUGHTERS OF MR HARRY DALE

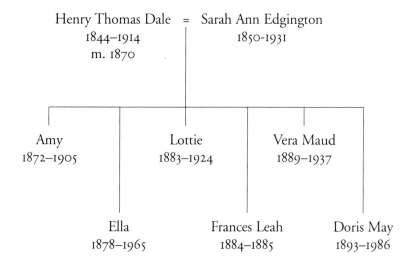

Henry Thomas Dale = Sarah Ann Edgington
1844–1914   1850-1931
m. 1870

Amy   Lottie   Vera Maud
1872–1905   1883–1924   1889–1937

Ella   Frances Leah   Doris May
1878–1965   1884–1885   1893–1986

THE SONS OF HARRY WAMBA DALE

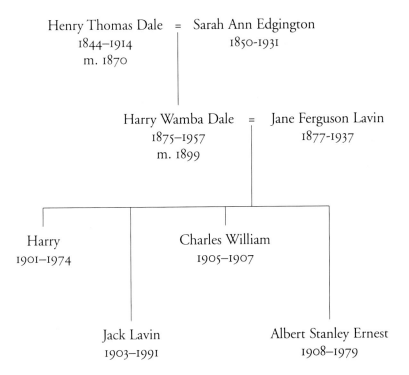

Henry Thomas Dale = Sarah Ann Edgington
1844–1914   1850-1931
m. 1870

Harry Wamba Dale = Jane Ferguson Lavin
1875–1957   1877-1937
m. 1899

Harry
1901–1974

Charles William
1905–1907

Jack Lavin
1903–1991

Albert Stanley Ernest
1908–1979

IN THE BEGINNING

The audience was restless with expectancy. There was not a seat to be had in the brand new auditorium as some 2,250 people waited impatiently for the evening to begin. They talked amongst themselves, the sound resonating around them while the members of the orchestra, dressed in evening clothes, took their seats. Tuning up took place noisily below the 1000 seat gallery which displayed the Royal Coat of Arms in the centre – a gold shield with a frieze in leather and gold in front of looped drapery. The audience could see the newly painted décor clearly thanks to over 300 gas burners pouring out a dazzling light throughout the arena. To pass the time they amused themselves looking for the dignitaries amongst the group of invited guests sitting in the stalls. The Lord Provost of the City of Edinburgh, Sir Thomas Clark and his wife were easily spotted amongst the other city magistrates, corporation guests and various invitees. Patronage by such distinguished guests meant the evening was special and all the spectators, regardless of background or social position, were aware of it.

For this was Monday, 8 November 1886 in the 49th year of the reign of Queen Victoria, and John Henry Cooke, entertainer, entrepreneur and showman was about to open his newly constructed Royal Circus in East Fountainbridge, Edinburgh.

At exactly 7.30 p.m. that winter evening, the circus ringmaster Mr J.P. Butler, immaculately attired in dark clothes, stepped into the arena amid loud cheers. With a nod from him, the orchestra, directed by Mr G. Spencer, gave a few bars of a familiar introduction to which the audience stood noisily, then in unison they sang the National Anthem. At its conclusion, and after the audience was seated again, a small, dapper man with a bushy dark moustache, stepped forward into the bright light of the circus ring. He was dressed as a traditional jester with cap and bells and had on a richly decorated brocade costume. The spectators were hushed as he raised his clear and powerful voice and recited with immaculate diction a prologue prepared by Mr Weston Gibb, John Henry Cooke's business manager. The prologue was short, embracing a welcome to the Royal Circus as well as a hope for an enjoyable occasion and as he concluded, there was a great cheer from the audience. The 'Court Jester', Mr Harry Dale, bowed and stepped back out of the circus ring.

Mr Harry Dale was my great grandfather and this opening performance by him launched John Henry Cooke's Royal Circus on an appreciative and enthusiastic Edinburgh audience. Cooke was a well-known figure in Edinburgh, born in New York in 1837 to English parents who were on tour at the time; he was a member of a large circus dynasty. The Cooke family had taken the circus concept, at one time regarded as a cheap and low level entertainment, to new heights of popularity with top class equestrianism, skilled jugglers, trapezists, gymnasts, vocalists, comics and clowns. They had been performing in Edinburgh for many years at

Palladium Theatre, 1971, formerly Cooke's Royal Circus, Edinburgh
(Kevin and Henry Wheelan/Edinburgh Central Library)

a number of locations throughout the city. By the 1880s Cooke's
Edinburgh Circus was a tented arena occupying ground in
Grindlay Street, below the castle and adjacent to Lothian Road, a
main thoroughfare in Edinburgh near to the west end of Princes
Street. But Cooke had to vacate the site when it was sold to the
theatrical entrepreneurs Howard & Wyndham, who built a new
theatre there and named it 'The Lyceum', opening it in 1883.

Cooke was not dismayed at this situation as he shrewdly bought
ground at East Fountainbridge, only a stone's throw away from
Lothian Road, and spent some £5,000 building a permanent circus
facility with increased comfort and seating and a flexible design to
allow the arena to be converted to a concert hall when the circus
season was over. Location was also important, as the bulk of the
circus goers were from the working class districts of the city. It was
adjacent to Tollcross and Earl Grey Street with their crowded three-
and four-storey tenements, and also close to the busy Grassmarket,
and the Cowgate with its immigrant Irish population, where escape
from unsanitary, overcrowded living conditions was provided by
the bright lights and cheerful programme.

My great grandfather came from a similar working-class
background in the industrial Midlands of England, so I am certain
he felt an empathy with the majority of the audience on that special
evening in 1886. He was aged 42 at the time but he was a seasoned
performer in the circus environment, and learned his trade before
that, on the stages of Victorian music halls in Britain, Ireland and
elsewhere.

Tracing a family tree these days has become simpler and more
satisfying thanks to the computer and the internet, plus a recognition by many authorities, public and private, that their archives
should be opened up to hungry and eager researchers. I launched
my family research with a clean sheet of paper. I knew nothing
about my ancestors, my father avoided the subject, and it was of no
concern until I had children of my own and I realised I wanted to
know where I had come from, so that I could pass the information
on to them in due course. I pressed my father hard when he turned
70 and he thought about it for a while then agreed to put pen to
paper. Once he got started his enthusiasm grew but I soon realised
why he had avoided talking about his early years for so long. It
emerged that he had had a very unhappy childhood; there were
many painful memories with which to deal. Sadly, a few months

after he started his recollections he became ill and needed major heart surgery, dying a few days later, a week before his 71st birthday. He had managed to write about the first 12 years of his life in some detail and amongst his memories was the intriguing comment, 'My grandfather was something in the circus although I never met him, and several of his children, including my father, were also involved.'

This was a catalyst for me to launch my research. My father's elder brother, Jack Dale, who lived in Birmingham but was born in Edinburgh, was still around and he came to my aid with much additional material, more memories and old photographs which gave some impetus to my investigations. I was determined from the start that the bare facts of births, marriages and deaths provided by the official certificates in the Register Offices of England and Scotland would be insufficient; I wanted to put flesh on the bones and find out as much as I could about my Dale ancestors.

John Henry Cooke's jester, 'Mr Harry Dale' was Henry Thomas Dale, born on 6 July 1844 in Baggot Street, Birmingham. The official birth certificate shows his father was named Henry Dale, a caster (journeyman foundryman), and his mother was Mary Anne Dale, maiden name Evans. They had married on 25 July 1842 at St Peter's Collegiate Church, Wolverhampton, a fine church near the town centre that is still in use to-day. (See p.5). Henry's father was William Dale, a locksmith, and Mary Anne's father was Thomas Evans, a labourer. Unfortunately, unlike the Scottish marriage certificates, the mothers of the newly weds were not mentioned. The first child of the marriage was William Dale born in May 1843 in Salop Street, Wolverhampton, but he died in June the same year. Henry Thomas Dale followed in 1844 but why he was born in Birmingham is not known as he was baptised in St Peter's Wolverhampton ten months later in May 1845 when the family was still living in Salop Street. He was the only child to survive as Henry and Mary Anne lost two further children, Rose Mary Dale, born and died in 1847, and Thomas Dale born 1849, died 1851. This little vignette of family life illustrates the high level of child mortality in Victorian times, especially in working-class areas.

Henry Dale, the father, appeared as a journeyman 'caster' or 'moulder' in various documents in keeping with the rapid development of engineering within Walsall, where he was born, and Wolverhampton, where he lived. I noted he was literate as he signed his marriage certificate whereas his wife, Mary Anne Dale, made a mark only as she could not write. Tracing the Dale family back another generation or two showed that they had origins in Stowe, an agricultural area in Staffordshire to the north-east of Wolverhampton. The industrial revolution forced more and more people from the rural areas into the towns and cities, and my Dale ancestors seemed to be good examples of this major social change.

Mary Anne Evans caused me a lot of problems as subsequent official documents showed 'Evans' was not her maiden name in spite of the marriage certificate entry that she was a spinster. Henry Dale, the caster, died of phthisis – lung disease, an occupational hazard in the foundry industry – aged only 32 in February 1852. He died at Little's Lane, Wolverhampton, and the informant listed on the death certificate was Elizabeth Rowlands. From the 1851 Wolverhampton census, she lived two or three doors away from the Dale family. Mary Anne Dale waited a few months and remarried in December 1852 to Henry George Claridge, a tailor. It was quite a common occurrence for widows and widowers to remarry, on the one hand to get a wage earner in the household, on the other to get

St Peter's Collegiate Church, Wolverhampton 2008 (Dale collection)

a woman to look after a house and children. On this marriage certificate she stated her maiden name as 'Rowlands' and her father was 'Thomas Rowlands'. The 1851 and 1861 censuses showed she had been born in Welshpool, Montgomeryshire, Wales, and lo and behold, the Rowlands family living nearby also came from the same county. With the help of the Powys Family History Society, I found Thomas and Elizabeth Rowlands married in 1818 and their first child, born in 1819 was named Mary Anne Rowlands. She was born on a farm named Trelydan near Guilsfield, a rural parish close to Welshpool. The family seem to have relocated from Montgomeryshire to the Midlands about the early 1840s. The puzzle is why Mary Anne gave the name 'Evans' on marrying Henry Dale in 1842. Perhaps she had been married before but I have not yet found any evidence to support such a marriage in Wales or England. However, on the 1851 census the name 'John Dale', son, aged eight appears alongside Henry Thomas Dale, son, aged six. As she lost a child in 1843 – William Dale – John Dale could not have been born that year and I can only postulate that John Dale was a love child of Mary Anne, probably born before her marriage to Henry Dale, and was adopted into the family on marrying Henry Dale, and his birth was probably not registered.

These facts are confusing but the history of my family is not straightforward, as this continuing story will reveal in due course.

I know little about the early childhood of my great grandfather, but I think he had a reasonable education as he could read and write and at some stage was apprenticed as a 'file-cutter'. In the 1861 census for Wolverhampton, aged 16, that is the description the enumerator gave him, which he used himself in future years. Losing his natural father when he was aged eight must have been traumatic, and when he was replaced by a step-father in his formative years this was no doubt difficult as well. But the 1861 census revealed that his mother, Mary Anne Claridge, was now described as a widow and Henry Thomas had lost his second father. Mary Anne now took the plunge yet again and married for the third time in St George's Church, Wolverhampton, on 12 May 1862 to John Corrock, a bachelor, two years younger than she and also a tailor. He was the son of James Corrock, a robe maker, and seemed to have his origins in the London area.

Jumping ahead to August 1901, when Henry Thomas Dale ('Mr Harry Dale') was performing at the Alhambra Circus in Blackpool, he was interviewed by 'Leo' of the *Blackpool Times* who asked for details of his early life. Harry Dale responded by saying he had a good voice as a boy and sang in the church choir of St Thomas' Church, Birmingham. Later, his voice changed to a powerful baritone and his parents moved to London enabling him to commence his career on the stage by getting engagements in small music halls such as Winingales in Whitechapel, and the Old Raglan in Theobolds Road.

Unfortunately, with three sets of parents, he did not specify which ones moved to London, but my conjecture is that John Corrock, with his existing London connections, was the most likely. I am also positing that someone recognised a talent in him and encouraged him to move away from the dirty, back-breaking toil of a file cutter, and seek pastures new on the music hall stage. Whether that person was of his family or a stranger will never be known but the change in his lifestyle was significant and ever lasting. Although he continued to describe himself as a 'file-cutter' even as late as 1875, on my grandfather's birth certificate, he had become an established music-hall entertainer by 1870.

Henry Thomas Dale, 'Mr Harry Dale', about 1885 (Dale Collection)

FUN AND GAMES IN REAL LIFE

Tracing the life of Henry Thomas Dale has involved recourse to several official documents supplemented by researching a number of publications in which he featured. The exact date when he moved from being an engineer working in Wolverhampton to London where his transformation to entertainer took place is not known. There are no family papers giving such vital information, since many photos, papers, letters, handbills, posters and other memorabilia of his life, and that of his family, were destroyed in a house fire and no biography of his career has ever been written that I have been able to trace. But by bringing together all the strands I have collected over the years, a tapestry has been woven which I think gives a reasonable idea of his life, both private and public. Whilst the results may shock in some aspects and delight in others, I have always reminded myself that he was living in difficult times with no welfare state to fall back on when times were hard, when the music hall was highly competitive with many artistes of varied talents fighting for recognition, and when self belief and perhaps an over-inflated ego were essential ingredients for success.

An official certificate dated 10 July 1864 shows the marriage of Henry Thomas Dale, aged 20, a file cutter living at Bilston Street, Wolverhampton to Emma Davis, aged 19, a shop girl from Walsall Street in the same town. They married in St George's Church and Henry Thomas' father was listed as Henry Dale, a moulder, while Emma's father was John Davis, a locksmith. The witnesses were Henry Davis, her brother, and Elizabeth Davis, his wife. [This marriage was about two years after the third marriage of his mother to John Corrock.] The newly weds seemed to have moved in with her father and mother as their first child, Rosanna Dale, was born about a year later in 1865 at Dudley Street in Wolverhampton, where John and Sarah Davis, her parents, were domiciled but this child died about three years later in 1868. A second child, Charles

Dale, followed in 1868 while a third, Sarah Ann Dale, was born in 1870 and baptised in April 1871. Perhaps this idyllic scene of family life has some appeal, but all was not as it seems.

I have mentioned above that I have not been able to find convincing evidence when Harry decided to turn from humble file cutter to entertainer. I have often wondered, though, if he was influenced by a writer in Victorian times who achieved great international success through the publication of a book entitled 'Self Help'. Samuel Smiles (1812–1904) the author, was born in Haddington near Edinburgh, and published his book in 1859. It was an immediate success as it illustrated how many individuals of humble origins, by determination and will power, achieved success in a range of occupations such as engineering, medicine, and the military life. Smiles had some key observations he used such as: 'The spirit of self help is the root of all genuine growth in the individual'; 'The reason so little is done is generally because so little is attempted'; and most significantly, 'Life will always be to a large extent what we ourselves make it.' I am theorising that Henry Thomas Dale read this book at some time in his early life and resolved to put into practice some of the lessons advocated by Samuel Smiles.

The first printed evidence I have of Henry Thomas Dale on the music hall stage is an advertisement on page 16 of *The Era,* a weekly newspaper published in London, dated 18 July 1869, showing that he was performing at the Scotia Music Hall, Stockwell Street, Glasgow. I was immediately struck by the positive image he painted of himself. This man was not a humble, modest individual, but someone proud of his achievements, and anxious that the entertainment world should know about him.

SCOTIA MUSIC HALL, Glasgow

Immense success of Harry Dale, comic vocalist and author of the following songs: 'The Pink Umbrella', (sung only by Will Hully), 'When George III was King', 'Happy Sam', 'The New Velocipede', 'King of Jollity', 'Honest Sons of Toil' 'A Vagabond's Life for Me', 'The New ABC'. Copies may be had for 18 stamps. Will be at the Southminster Music Hall, Edinburgh July 26th. To follow: Greatbridge, Coventry, (5th engagement), Dublin, etc Letters addressed as above. Vacant dates September 6th, three weeks, October 4th, one month.

The following week, he was indeed appearing in the Southminster Music Hall in Edinburgh [a location now occupied by the Edinburgh Festival Theatre]. An advertisement on the front page of *The Scotsman* on Tuesday 27 July placed by the proprietor, Mr Levy, describes Harry Dale as a 'comic vocalist' whilst the report of the opening performance praises 'Mr Harry Dale as a good buffo singer ...'

As seemed to be his habit, he bought more space on page 16 of *The Era* of 1 August 1869 and boasted:

SOUTHMINSTER MUSIC HALL, Edinburgh

Harry Dale has another great hit at the above hall, receiving the plaudits of delighted thousands for his great buffo and original comic songs. He does not only sing but writes good songs such as 'When George III was King', 'Honest Sons of Toil', 'Newmarket Jack' or 'The Pride of my Life is the Pigskin', 'Jolly Joe', 'King of Jollity', 'The World Turned Upside Down', etc etc

Engagements as follows: Glasgow, Greatbridge, Dublin, Wear Music Hall, Sunderland, Coventry, etc. At liberty October 4th. Letters addressed as above.

These items indicate to me that he was already touring the country building up his experience and reputation while, presumably, his wife Emma was back home with her parents in Wolverhampton, looking after the family.

A new development caused me some anguish. I had researched backwards from my grandfather, christened Harry Dale, who was born in 1875 in Oldham, and looking at his birth certificate, found that Henry Thomas Dale, file cutter, was indeed his father, but his mother was Ada Dale, née Edgington. My initial reaction was that his first wife, Emma, must have died, probably in childbirth, and he had quickly married again as he needed a woman to look after his children, a not uncommon feature of Victorian Britain. How wrong I was!

I could not find any marriage for Dale and Edgington in the

English General Register Office indexes for the period 1870 to 1880. Knowing that he was touring the country visiting provincial music halls in Scotland as well as England, I then looked at the marriage register in Scotland, and there it was. On 26 September 1870 Henry Thomas Dale, a 'vocalist' married Sarah Ann Edgington, also a 'vocalist', at St Mary's Scottish Episcopalian Church, Renfrew Street, Glasgow. The marriage certificate states his father was Henry Dale, a caster, and his mother was Mary Anne Dale. Researching the local Glasgow newspapers and copies of *The Era* – a valuable source of information about music-hall performances throughout the UK – showed that a dancer named Ada Cooke was performing in the Scotia Music Hall, while Mr Harry Dale was performing at the Britannia Music Hall, both well established places of entertainment in Glasgow. Sarah Ann Edgington's mother's maiden name was 'Cooke' and the family came from Liverpool, so I think she used 'Ada Cooke' as a stage name. He was 26 at the time, and said he was a bachelor, while she was 18, and a spinster.

This situation had to be further investigated and recourse to the 1871 census showed his legal wife Emma Dale was hale and hearty, still living in Wolverhampton with her parents at Pountney Folds, Dudley Street, with her children Charles and Sarah Ann Dale listed. Meanwhile, Henry Thomas Dale and his 'wife' Ada Dale were listed at 18 Picton Street in Newcastle where he was performing for two weeks at the Oxford Music Hall. He was described in the census as a 'professional singer' while Ada Dale was a 'professional dancer'. I had no choice but to assume he had committed bigamy!

There are two official sources in London that hold details of 'Decrees Absolute', i.e. recognised official divorces granted in England and Wales. The National Archives at Kew has an index which can be searched online but they had no details of a divorce for Dale–Davis. Her Majesty's Court Service, Principal Registry of the Family Division located at High Holborn, can also search for Decrees Absolute from 1858 to 1939. It received my search fee and searched from 1865 to 1874 and after a couple of weeks the reply came back that they had no record of a 'Decree Absolute' for Henry Thomas and Emma Dale during this period. This changed my whole attitude to my great grandfather overnight! I had up to that point regarded him as someone who dragged himself and his family out of a poverty trap by hard work and dedication. I have to assume

Sarah Ann Dale, née Edgington, on right hand side, with daughter Ella and son *c*.1916 (Dale Collection)

he either walked out on his wife and family in Wolverhampton as he developed his career, was totally indifferent to her, or perhaps he agreed with her that a mutual separation was required and hopefully supported her with money from time to time. I looked at the census returns for Wolverhampton from 1871 until 1911, the last one available at present, and Emma Dale was listed in every one, still practising as a 'tray polisher', but moving house from time to time as first her father died, then her mother. The most damning evidence, however, was still to come!

After his marriage to Sarah Ann Edgington in Glasgow, they had a child, Amy Dale, born in London in 1872 when he was performing for a few weeks at leading London music halls such as the Marylebone Music Hall in the High Street, and Sam Collin's Hall in Islington. After that period, they set up home in Oldham, Lancashire, where his first son Albert Dale was born in 1873, followed by his second son, Harry Dale – my grandfather – in 1875. On these birth certificates he describes himself, not as a music-hall artist, but as a 'file cutter', his original occupation in Wolver-hampton. Then lo and behold, Emma Dale, his legal wife, had a son named John Dale in May 1876 in Wolverhampton and that birth certificate states the father was Henry Thomas Dale, a 'file-cutter'! Was he really the father? Did he return to her for a night or two of passion or was Emma Dale enjoying herself safe in the knowledge that she had a ready made husband to cover any of her dalliances? Further research revealed that John Dale was baptised in St Peter's Church, Wolverhampton, in October 1876, that is, five months later. The interesting fact was that only Emma Dale's name was entered in the baptismal register column headed 'Parents Name'. There was no mention of Henry Thomas Dale as the father, nor was any other male name entered. I have concluded that Henry Thomas Dale was probably not the father – John Dale's father was someone else. I think she entered Henry Thomas Dale's name on the official register to legitimise her son for later life, but as she lived in St Peter's parish, the real father may have been known to the parish priest and others, and so she refused to enter his name in the register. I will never know the true facts.

Forced to put aside his private life, I followed his music-hall career by researching a number of appropriate local newspapers and the weekly publications *The Era,* and *The Stage. The Era* continued this valuable service up to 1939 when it ceased publication. Each week it gave details of the shows at the theatres, circuses and music halls throughout England, Scotland, Wales, Ireland and often theatres in other parts of the Empire. It listed the owners of the premises, the entertainers and their acts, and gave a brief comment about their individual performances ranging from 'capital' at one end of the spectrum, to 'could do better' at the other end. I was also fortunate to get a lot of additional information from *The Stage,* which had been thoroughly examined by a distant relative who was also researching our family. We pooled resources and results and he provided many further pieces in the jigsaw that were the career and family of Henry Thomas Dale.

Unfortunately, *The Era* has yet to be transferred in total onto searchable CDs, or online, so my initial research involved scanning by eye some 80 to 100 entries each week seeking the name, or names, I was looking for. It was tedious work and could be described as character building, but I found my eye gradually became accustomed to the job, and I was amazed sometimes at how much information leapt off the page. However human it is to err, I think I have nonetheless identified a high percentage of 'mentions' of Harry Dale, and later, members of his family. Around 2008 the distant relative mentioned above, who is more computer literate than I, did discover a website linked to the Newspaper Section of the British Library in London where *The Era* could be searched online up to 1900. He provided me with reams of references, many of which I had already, but including some that helped to flesh out the bare bones.

My research covered a period from 1865 to 1914 in Harry Dale's case, and took me some six years to complete. However, it was satisfying in many ways and also gave me an insight into the nomadic existence of entertainers in Victorian and Edwardian times when stage contracts might only be for a week or two in each location, with a possible bonus of a few weeks over the Christmas/New Year period, if they were lucky. The other fascination for me was the realisation that communication between the actors/entertainers and theatre/music-hall management was essentially by letter, or 'wire', which I realised was actually a telegram in modern parlance. The system seems to have been remarkably efficient in contrast with our current mail system with e-mail and telephone now replacing the 'wire'.

I was also impressed at just how hard all these entertainers, had to work. Two performances an evening was standard fare with the odd matinee thrown in as well. Harry Dale travelled the length and breadth of Britain and Ireland with, for example over a four-week period, a week in Grimsby, then Birmingham, then Leeds and finally South Shields. From the 1850s onwards, the railway network throughout Britain expanded at an amazing speed, opening up the country for travellers and I am certain the entertainment profession were good and regular customers.

Monday seemed to be rehearsal day at most music-hall establishments, followed by an evening performance; then one or two shows a night for the rest of the week and possibly a matinee on the Saturday. I noted that later in Harry's life, around Christmas and New Year, circus entertainers in particular were expected to perform three or four times a day! Many music-hall and circus entertainers used agents to find engagements but I have only sketchy evidence that Harry Dale used one and that was mainly in his early days on the stage. He certainly advertised his experience and success frequently in the press, and seemed to have plenty of engagements for all the years I researched him.

Sunday allowed him to return to his home and prepare for the next week's travels. In some cases, he managed to organise a proper circuit such as a week performing in Glasgow, then a steamer to Belfast for the next week, a train down to Dublin for the next week and finally the steamer from Dublin across to Liverpool for his final week, completing the circuit back in England. Perhaps the reason he 'married' a fellow entertainer in Glasgow was because she would understand the sort of life he had to have to achieve success, whereas his legal wife in Wolverhampton, an unremarkable tray polisher all her working life, perhaps found it difficult to comprehend the forces that drove him forward. I am not making excuses for his behaviour, but trying to understand who he was, and why he did what he did.

After his 'marriage' in Glasgow in September 1870, he spent the next couple of months touring the provincial music halls in the north of England. Many of these halls are now either forgotten or have been renamed. It is perhaps worth mentioning that several called themselves 'music halls' but were, in fact, glorified public houses with a large room housing a stage and a critical audience which would soon let the entertainer know if he or she was acceptable. He visited Scarborough (the Prince of Wales Music

Hall), Liverpool (the Adelphi Music Hall), Oldham, (also the Adelphi) and the People's Hall in Manchester, arriving there at Christmas 1870. At this point, another talent emerged. He placed an advertisement in *The Era* that week describing himself as 'buffo comic and author of new sensible songs ... sung by himself' naming them as 'The Ball Room Belles', 'No Such Luck for Me' and 'Under the Mistletoe'.

Just how and when did he learn to write music? Establishing himself on the stage was hard enough in a highly competitive environment, but mastering the art of musical composition and writing words to the tunes was quite an achievement for a man of such humble origins. I have managed to acquire about five of his published music-hall songs from sources such as the Bodleian Library in Oxford, and the British Library Music Section in London and it is quite clear from the sheet music covers that he composed the music as well as the lyrics. There was collaboration in some cases but that does not detract from the fundamental fact that he was a true professional musical entertainer. I think it is also fair to say that there was a huge range of music-hall songs written in this period by many artistes. In broadly categorising them, many were sentimental or romantic ballads, but there were also a number of bawdy songs entwining innuendo into the words. The eagle eye of the Lord Chamberlain tried to keep order but many songs escaped his censorious blue pencil. Mr Harry Dale wrote in both genres, but I am glad to report his two most famous songs were romantic ballads and one, entitled 'Silver Bells of Memory', written in the 1880s, was still available as sheet music published in 1932. I suppose he gauged his audience as artistes do today, and selected the songs to suit the occasion. A goodly percentage of women in the audience would respond to his romantic renditions, whereas a noisy, drunken group of working men having a good time would perhaps have appreciated a more suggestively worded song. There is evidence that he wrote over 300 songs but only a handful have survived.

By February 1871 he was back in Scotland performing in Aberdeen at MacFarland's Grand Music Hall; Leith (the port of Edinburgh) at the Royal Music Hall; and Paisley at the Royal Exchange Rooms. Another advert in *The Era* for early February lists all his engagements throughout Britain for many weeks ahead describing himself as 'Buffo and Comic' and the subsequent write-

ups by the critics provided him with several quotes such as a 'capital
comic', 'merited applause', 'genuine comic vocalist' and so on.

By the start of 1872 he had toured many of the local halls of
Britain and again he chose to advertise himself in *The Era* on 28
January:

Leeds, HOBSON'S

Harry Dale, Buffo and comic extraordinary whose success
is so great at the above he is actually cheered nightly. Re-
engaged for two weeks longer. No vacancy for the provinces
this year (nor any other year for Scotland). Adelphi,
Oldham, February 12th. London, May 6th. Agent: Fred
Abrahams.

After a further few weeks touring the halls of northern England he
set off in early May for an important series of engagements in
London. Any entertainer invited to perform in the capital must
have felt some trepidation, as well as exultation that all his hard
work in the previous months on the provincial circuit had received
recognition. His singing talent – a fine baritone voice – was noted
throughout his career, his writing and composing of many original
songs, his comic abilities and his success in making an audience
laugh and enjoy themselves, were the key factors in his career.

LONDON AND ELSEWHERE

The history of the theatre in Britain gives a fascinating glimpse of the changing social and political conditions within which it sought to operate. The restoration of King Charles II in 1660 revived the theatre which had ceased to prosper under Cromwell's Puritan Commonwealth. Charles granted 'patents' to selected theatres in London and others outside of London giving rise to the 'Theatre Royal' concept allowing serious drama to be performed. For example, the Theatre Royal in London's Drury Lane received its patent in 1662, whilst the Theatre Royal in York paid £500 for a patent in 1769. The patent was jealously guarded by those patentees fortunate enough to hold one. The theatrical performances continued throughout the 17th and 18th centuries but there was a definite change in mood amongst the population by the time Queen Victoria mounted the throne in 1837. Factors included attendance dropping due to difficult economic times; the move from countryside into urban environment by thousands of people catalysed by the industrial revolution; and the development of the railway system which was now providing travel opportunities. The patent situation determined the restricted programmes put on at theatres, while the non-patent establishments, to keep within the law, provided poor quality drama sometimes interspersed with music and singing. The Lord Chamberlain was the licensing authority, ensuring all was controlled and censored appropriately.

There was, however, a major change when the Theatres Act of 1843 removed the principle of the patent theatres, allowing the Lord Chamberlain to grant a licence to any suitable person. The pubs and saloon bar owners were not slow to grasp the opportunity and recognised a new type of customer – men and women seeking light entertainment and an enjoyable night out – and being good marketeers the owners tried to match the demand. The seeds of the British music hall had been sown.

The need in London for new purpose-built premises to satisfy the demand for what we now call 'light entertainment' was high. In 1851 the Sun Music Hall in the High Street, Knightsbridge was built to seat some 800 patrons. Originally it was the Rising Sun pub, and the new premises were built behind it. In 1855 a budding entrepreneur named Charles Morton built the Canterbury Music Hall adjacent to his Lambeth located pub and never looked back. Other pub owners watched carefully and a series of large establishments were created throughout London. Examples included the Marylebone Music Hall, Marylebone High Street (1856); the Bedford Music Hall in Camden High Street (1861), the Metropolitan Music Hall, Edgware Road (1862) and Collin's Music Hall, Islington Green (1862). There were many others in London such as the South London Palace, The Royal Music Hall, Middlesex Music Hall and New Star Music Hall. Elsewhere in Britain, similar styles of music halls sprang into life such as the 1,000 seat Britannia in the Trongate, Glasgow (c.1858), the London Museum Concert Hall, Digbeth, Birmingham (1863) and many more, in all the principal cities of England, Scotland, Wales and Ireland.

The programme on offer in most of these establishments was a mixture of vocalists, serious and comic, male and female; comedians; dancers; gymnasts; jugglers; male/female impersonators; clog dancers; animal acts such as dogs and monkeys; strongmen; tight rope walkers; trapeze artists; and a host of other unusual acts. The patrons were quite critical and high-spirited, and when fuelled with alcohol were not averse to shouting their appreciation or booing their disfavour.

Into this cauldron in 1872 stepped Harry Dale, still a relative newcomer to the business, and more used to the provincial music-hall circuit where his Midlands accent was better understood and his songs were perhaps more relevant to the audience. He arrived in London in May 1872 and performed from May until July in the Marylebone Music Hall. The proprietor of the music hall at that time was Mr R.F. Bottings, a man with a fierce reputation who competed hard with the other music-hall owners to bring in the audiences. He put together a mixed programme including 'Mr & Mrs Hemfrey, popular duettists; Wainratta, a marvellous performer on the wire; Miss Florrie Seaman, comedienne; Tom Laburnum – 'who's homely and chaste pathos is quite touching'; Mr Tom McLean a comic; and of course, Mr Harry Dale variously described as 'topic vocalist and author', 'comic basso', 'motto song singer' and 'comical exponent of nigger eccentricities' [no Race Relations Act in these days]. Not being one to hide himself in the background, Harry Dale placed an advert in *The Era* on 9 and 16 June 1872 modestly claiming:

> Mr Harry Dale is one of the most successful versatile vocalists that ever appeared in London. Author of 'The Green Umbrella Belles', 'It's an Ill-Wind Blows Nobody Good', 'It's a Long Lane that Never has a Turning'. Terrific shouts of applause.
>
> MARYLEBONE 8.45
>
> SAM COLLIN'S 10.10

This advert, besides naming some of his early songs, showed he was determined to make the most of his time in London, and earn money. After performing at the Marylebone at 8.45 p.m., he dashed off to Sam Collin's Music Hall at Islington Green, and was on stage there at 10.10 p.m. On modern maps, these two locations are not exactly close together, so allowing for a 15/20 minutes performance at the Marylebone, he only had an hour to get to Islington and prepare himself for his second performance. Perhaps he had a horse-drawn cab waiting outside the Marylebone to take him direct or possibly the Metropolitan Underground line opened in 1863 gave him a flying start from one music hall to the other. Regardless, it must have been a tiring exercise.

His 1872 stay in London concluded at the end of July where one review in *The Era* states 'A large share of the holiday pocket money has flowed into the coffers of Mr Botting's popular little hall for here has been presented entertainment which will bear comparison with that presented in more pretentious halls ... Mr Harry Dale shone in what are called motto songs ...' and again: 'Of the unabated popularity of this pleasant place of amusement evidence is to be found in the large audiences which continue to assemble notwithstanding the warm weather ... a Negro entertainment was given by Mr Harry Dale who wound up with a diverting parody of the ballad "Driven From Home".'

London was also the place where Harry Dale's first child to his 'second' wife was born. Amy Dale arrived in July, the first of 11 children borne by Sarah Ann Edgington, the vocalist and dancer he had married in Glasgow two years before. It would seem that they moved around together presumably either renting a house, or staying at 'theatrical digs' as other Dale children appear later at locations throughout England where he was performing.

After his successful sojourn in London he returned north appearing in August at the Britannia Music Hall in the Trongate, Glasgow. This very popular establishment is one of the few mid-19th-century music halls in Britain that has survived. Its Italianate façade on the Trongate, near George Square, was positioned above a modern amusement arcade for many years until 'discovered' again in the late 1990s by a group of enthusiasts. It is slowly being restored to its former glory. Although featured in the BBC 'Restoration' series, it was not successful in getting financial support but is now living again as a theatre of entertainment. Under the enthusiastic guidance of Judith Bowers and The Friends of the Britannia Panopticon (of which I am a member) this delightful little theatre is part of my family's history, as well as Glasgow's and Britain's. (See p.38).

October and November 1872 saw Harry Dale in residence at Thornton's Varieties in Leeds. The early music halls often took the name of the proprietor, as this one did, but to the people of modern day Leeds, it is now the City Varieties. Again, this is a great and beautiful survivor of the music-hall era where any visitor can savour the atmosphere of old time music hall. This theatre featured on TV several years ago where all the acts were introduced, in traditional Victorian style, by a 'Chairman' who kept the programme moving, and whose other principal task was to keep the audience calm!

An unusual challenge was noted in *The Era* of 29 September when a Mr W.W. Whitlock challenged Harry Dale to sing against him a comic and a sentimental song for the sum of £10; Mr Dale to choose time and place if he accepted the challenge.

Harry Dale utilised the columns of *The Era* again on 20 October 1872 to issue a response as follows:

VARIETIES MUSIC HALL, Leeds.

Mr Harry Dale will accept W. Whitlock's Challenge to sing one comic and one sentimental song for £10 a side and has placed £1 in the hands of Mr Marchant, Theatre Royal, Wakefield, where the contest will take place first week in December or at Mechanics Hall, Hull, last week in December or first week in January. Mr Dale will sing a sentimental song against any recognised comic vocalist in Great Britain for from £10 to £50 a side.

Mr W.W. Whitlock, described as a 'comedian, vocalist and mimic' replied on 12 January 1873 stating he had never been to Hull or Wakefield where he knew Mr D. was a favourite, so he suggested any music hall in London or the provinces. Once more Mr D. replied that the only vacant date he had in 1873 was 17 March but W.W. Whitlock opted out of the whole exercise by saying in an advert of 19 January that he was engaged that week. As far as I know, this to and fro challenge never reached fruition but did seem to provide both entertainers with cheap publicity, and probably considerable amusement to other music-hall entertainers.

It did show that Harry Dale was not averse to spending some money on rather complex announcements in a widely distributed entertainment paper. Some might say he was arrogant, but as I have commented before, he was in a cut-throat business and self-confidence and self-aggrandisement were probably essential character traits.

In the middle of this challenge match his wife, Sarah Ann, gave birth to their first boy, Albert Dale, who arrived in February 1873 at their house in Oldham, Lancashire. Albert, true to his genes, was destined for the entertainment business in later life.

The year 1873 passed rapidly with appearances throughout the country, and in early 1874 he was back in London at the Canterbury Music Hall followed by the Royal where he performed a special act as 'The Ashantee Warrior'. The Ashanti Wars started in April 1873 in the Gold Coast, now known as Ghana, in West Africa, where the British army under Wolseley eventually defeated the Ashanti in January 1874 and burnt their capital, Kumasi. Harry Dale was obviously appealing to the patriotism of his audiences and showed a shrewd recognition that his topical act would be well publicised. After a couple of weeks in Hull he returned to London in April and at the South London Palace performed his 'Ashantee Warrior' act again.

He favoured the northern music halls for the rest of that year and at the beginning of 1875, his second son, baptised Harry Dale, was born in Oldham. He was my grandfather, and like his older brother Albert, also became an entertainer.

Harry Dale's next appearances in London took place in the summer of 1875 and they were well advertised in *The Era* when on 20 June a brief insert on page 16 stated:

> Mr Harry Dale
> *The great baritone comique*
>
> Will shortly make his first appearance in London at
> THE OXFORD, THE BEDFORD and THE SUN.

At the foot of the advert an agent 'Charles Roberts' is mentioned and he presumably placed the ad. At this stage in his career, Harry Dale must have found it useful to have a London agent, when most of his success had been in the provincial music-hall circuits in the north of England, Scotland and Ireland.

Further adverts followed with a mention on 4 July in *The Era,* under the heading of 'The Bedford Music Hall, Camden, Proprietor Mr Alfred Trotman', that Monday 5 July would see the first appearance of Harry Dale, 'the great provincial comique'.

Although he is listed in the programmes for the Sun on 11, 18 and 25 July, the Bedford on 18 July, and the Metropolitan on 1 August, there is virtually no praiseworthy comment about his performances. I have no evidence to support my supposition that all was not well with these repeat appearances on the London music-hall circuit, but to the best of my knowledge his future performances in the capital were few and far between. He seemed more at ease with northern audiences whose humour was perhaps more earthy and in tune with his background. I do not think he was unique in this, as several northerners over the years up to comparative modern times attempted to break into the London scene but were not a success. Some did climb over the barrier like Harry Lauder, Arthur Lloyd, Vesta Tilley and so on, but many returned to their roots and I think Harry Dale fell into that category.

After London he had a full programme of performances in Leeds, Sheffield, Birmingham, Nottingham, Barnsley, Hudders-field, Oldham and Hull to complete the year of 1875, gathering positive comments on the way such as 'an excellent comic'; 'a baritone and author of his own songs who gives great satisfaction'; 'a very clever comic singer'; and 'his comic effusions take immensely' illustrating the use of English as an art form by this particular critic perhaps seeking a higher position than a humble reporter of music-hall acts!

The year 1876 was very similar in that he moved round the northern part of the country performing in locations such as Great Grimsby, Leeds, Bolton, Bradford, Ashton under Lyme and Hull where he seemed to be a particular favourite at both the Alhambra Palace Hall and the Mechanics Music Hall.

As previously mentioned, I was rather taken aback by the birth in Wolverhampton to Emma Dale, his 'legitimate' wife of a boy, John Dale, on 6 May 1876. The name of Henry Thomas Dale, 'a file cutter', appears on the official birth certificate and a local researcher, on my behalf, managed to find the baptismal entry for the same John Dale in St Peter's Church, Wolverhampton in October 1876 with no father noted in the appropriate column in the church register. Again as noted earlier, I do not think Henry Thomas Dale was the natural father. Emma Dale was now 31 years old, and Henry Thomas Dale was 32.

In early 1877 he was performing in Bolton at James Pullan's Theatre of Varieties and a week later on 15 January Harry and Sarah Ann had a fourth child and third boy born in the Prestwich area of Manchester, and he was named Ernest Dale. Again, Harry Dale described himself as a 'file cutter' on the birth certificate. Ernest chose to bypass the bright lights of the stage and joined the Royal Navy in later life.

It is worth mentioning that a local paper, *The Hull Packet & East Riding Times*, reported a fund-raising concert for Hull Infirmary in March 1877 where Harry Dale participated, reflecting a charitable streak in his character. Another example was his listing as a contributor – albeit a modest one – to a fund for the relief of 'the late Price Barnes during his long illness, and for his mother to assist her in paying funeral expenses'. I assume Price Barnes was another music-hall performer, and from the extensive list of published donations in October 1877, was a popular individual. I think there is sufficient evidence that Great Grandfather did involve himself in certain charitable events over the many years he was a performer and in these times, where there was no welfare state to

fall back on, it was a common occurrence to support fellow professionals.

It emerged that 1878 was another busy year for Harry Dale but
it would be tedious to enumerate his many appearances throughout
England, Scotland, Wales and Ireland. One advert he placed in *The
Era* in late September is worth mentioning, however, and it is a
paraphrased letter as follows:

BRITANNIA MUSIC HALL, Glasgow. September 23rd 1878

Mr Harry Dale:
'Dear Sir, After an absence of five years from this establishment, I beg to compliment you on receiving the most
hearty reception accorded to any artist who appeared this
evening. I also must thank you for so kindly responding to
the sixth encore. Wishing you continuance of this unique
success, I am etc H.T. Rossborough, Proprietor'

This seems a rather unusual compliment paid to him by a well
known Glasgow music-hall proprietor. Harry Dale, to use the Scots
expression, had 'a guid conceit of himself' and published it for all
to see. Presumably Mr Rossborough approved and Harry Dale
continued to appear in the 'Brit' for many years to come.

He followed up with a further advert in the same paper dated
13 October 1878 where he states:

Mr Harry Dale, Buffo and Comic Vocalist still holds his
position as second to none in his line. Greatest success ever
achieved in Glasgow. Commencing booking for next year.
Voice: brilliant as ever; songs better; topic, comic, ballad
and national.

On 29 December 1878, Harry and Sarah Ann's fifth child and
second daughter named Ella was born at 11 Lawrence Street,
Sunderland, Co. Durham. The birth in Sunderland was
noteworthy as he was performing for several weeks at the 'New
Wear Music Hall', an establishment owned by Mr Stuart Henry
Bell. The occasion was a novel entertainment described as 'The
Adventures of the Terrible Pirate Schooner Stella' where an adver-
tisement describes a 'masterpiece of stage marine painting and

mechanical inventions' representing a journey and eventual destruction by explosion of the pirate ship. Mr Harry Dale was contracted as 'cicerone' – a wonderful old word meaning a guide – to describe the pictures alongside other music-hall entertainers from the opening of the show in December 1878 to its final performances in February 1879.

In a sense the proprietor, Stuart Henry Bell, was prescient in providing moving dioramas, as the music halls and circuses later in the century realised they were competing with the newly developed moving pictures, initially called 'biographs', and so embraced them such that it became quite normal for films to be run towards the end of an evening's entertainment. However, this response to public demand eventually became a Trojan Horse forecasting the decline and demise of the music hall in the 20th century, as the cinema became the principal means of entertaining the masses.

In his familiar modest manner, Harry Dale's advert in *The Era* of 2 March 1879 states:

> I, Harry Dale, beg publicly to thank Mr H. Rossborough, Glasgow, and Mr H.E. Moss, Edinburgh, for altering dates of my engagements, enabling me to return to the Wear, Sunderland, for a month, June 2nd, where I have concluded 66 nights in which time I have sung 334 songs, or an average of more than 5 each night, and never missing one or more curtains, besides 62 times describing Mr Bell's grand work of art 'The Pirate Schooner Stella'. Allowed by the proprietor, public and press to be the finest speaker in the Concert Halls. Return again to the Wear for 3 months December 15th. Author and composer of Graham & McBryde's 'Awkward Squad'.

Rossborough was the same proprietor of the Britannia in Glasgow, whilst Moss was developing his future music-hall success as a proprietor of the Empire Palace Theatre in Edinburgh. The Moss Empires became a huge and profitable conglomerate throughout the British Isles by the end of the 19th century and well into the 20th.

There seems no doubt from this and other comments over the years that Harry Dale had a voice that carried and he was blessed with good diction and pronunciation. Whether he had lost his

Midlands accent is not known, but in a period where performers on the stage and elsewhere were not assisted by microphones and loudspeakers, it must have been quite an achievement to sing five songs a night and provide a descriptive dialogue of the unique entertainment provided in the Wear Music Hall.

During the time and commitment he made to the Wear Music Hall over a three-month period, it was probably the sensible thing to rent a house in Sunderland and live there while Sarah Ann had her fifth child, and looked after the couple's other four children.

After his sojourn in Sunderland, he returned to the music-hall circuit in the north performing in Sheffield, Nottingham and Bradford before returning to the Britannia in Glasgow in May 1879 for a couple of weeks. The reporter for *The Era* in Glasgow stated:

> Mr Harry Dale, the deservedly popular baritone and buffo vocalist commenced a short engagement on Monday evening and met with the reception due to so old a favourite. Business, as might be expected with such excellent company, is now first class.

After Glasgow he was back at the Wear in June, then followed that with Carlisle before returning to his birthplace, Birmingham, where he performed for two weeks at the quaintly named London Museum Concert Hall.

This music hall was in the Bullring at the corner of Digbeth and Park Street, close to St Martin's Church and Moore Street Railway Station. It was built at a cost of £7,000 and was opened on 24 December 1863 by the respected proprietor, George Biber. It could hold 900 people inside its simple rectangular shape and was a favourite with the local working-class population. Part of it has survived into the 21st century, but only the shell of the building, which is now located opposite the new Selfridges Store, and from the outside, it looks rather small. Latterly it was fronted by the Royal George public house, but that has closed and I can only hope that the carcase of a grand old Victorian music hall can defy the odds and survive a bit longer. (See p.46).

Harry Dale performed there for two weeks and as was his custom, broadcast his talents in *The Era* on 14 September 1879:

> Harry Dale, the only comic baritone, writer and

composer of 300 songs, specially engaged, September
22nd, for the Prince of Wales Theatre, Wolverhampton,
in the great drama of 'After Dark'. First vacancy, April 5th
1880.

To me, the most fascinating feature of his latest advert was his
forthcoming appearance in the Prince of Wales Theatre in
Wolverhampton. Probably a place he was not keen to visit as his
legitimate wife was still living there with two Dale sons – Charles
and John. Perhaps he was tempted by the fee he could earn or
maybe he 'toughed it out' to use modern parlance. He would know
that Emma was illiterate, and possibly gambled she would not
know he was there at the theatre. Again, this is entirely conjecture
on my part, but it does create some intriguing possibilities.

He was in Wolverhampton for two weeks where the local report
stated: '… on Monday evening was produced a drama entitled
"The Scamps of London" or "The Cross Roads of Life" upon which
was founded Boucicalts "After Dark". In the music hall scene, the
Sisters Chellion, Demetri and Mr Harry Dale (a good comic)
appeared and were well received.'

Moving on from Wolverhampton he performed at
Southampton, Sheffield, Manchester, Edinburgh and Bradford
towards the end of 1879 before revisiting Glasgow and the Britannia
Music Hall in early 1880.

There are many references to Harry Dale's songs in the entertainment press during the years in which he performed. I have
trawled these and the collection of titles listed overleaf amounts to
only forty-eight. He claimed to have written over 300 during his
professional career, so the ones identified are about 15% of that
total. Many, no doubt, were forgettable and some were probably
dashed off to suit a particular occasion. In those days, up until the
1906 Musical Copyright Act, the enforcement of copyright was
difficult so little was published unless it was a really popular song,
or performed by the top rank of entertainers. Of those shown
overleaf, I have found the music and words for only five that were
published and have survived, and they are identified with an
asterisk, while some of the words for another three have been found
without music, and are given two asterisks. If anyone can add to
this list, I would be happy to hear from them. The 1870s and 1880s
were good decades for him – but he never reached the heights of

the likes of Dan Leno, Vesta Tilley, Marie Lloyd, Vesta Victoria, Harry Lauder, Arthur Lloyd and other Victorian household names.

A Vagabond's Life for Me
Absence of Mind
Alone I Did It*
Awkward Squad
Best of Friends Must Part
Bonnie Girl
Clean Your Boots
Do Not Forget
Does Thy Heart Beat True To Me*
Down by the Silvery Waters
Driven from Home
Happy Sam
Honest Sons of Toil
In Praise of the Ladies Fair**
It's an Ill Wind Blows Nobody Good
It's Awful
It Makes Me So Wild
It's a Long Lane that Never has a Turning
Jolly Joe
King of Jollity
Mistaken Identity*
My Waxwork Show
My Museum
Newmarket Jack
No Such Luck for Me
On My Honour it is True
Picking Pretty Shells
Pretty Little Sally**
Seaport Town
Silver Bells of Memory*
Some Mother's Boy
Squeeze My Little Finger*
Spooning the Bar
Sweet Seventeen**
Tell Me to My Face Like a Man
The Ball Room Belles
The Black Flag

The Doolan and Magee Wedding
The Green Umbrella Belles
The Heavy Man at the Vic
The Holy Friar
The New ABC
The New Velocipede
The Swell out of Luck
The Pink Umbrella
The World Turned Upside Down
Under the Mistletoe
When George III was King

In some instances he wrote the words and composed the music, while in other cases, I have found, he provided the words only, and someone else composed the music. Of the words that have survived, I have examined his two most popular romantic songs 'Does Thy Heart Beat True To Me' and 'Silver Bells of Memory' and whilst to modern eyes and mind they seem dated, there is no doubt they were romantic and nostalgic with a strong appeal to the female members of an audience in Victorian/Edwardian Britain. The first verse and chorus of 'Does Thy Heart Beat True To Me' are:

'Does thy heart beat true to me my love?'
I said when last we met.
Her eyes they shone like stars above,
Me thinks I see them yet.
Her bosom heaved a tender sigh,
She said 'Where'er I be,
Remember love until I die
My heart belongs to thee.'

In the silent night when the moon shines bright,
I am far upon the sea,
I'll ask thee love by the stars above,
'Does thy heart beat true to me?'

The note he has struck in this song is the remembered love when he or she is far away beyond the shores. A theme repeated in many songs through the ages, but always likely to raise a tear amongst an audience. Many born in Britain and Ireland in Victorian times did

SILVER BELLS OF MEMORY

SONG

Written
and
Composed
by

HARRY DALE

PRICE SIXPENCE

F. PITMAN HART & CO LTD.
20 & 21 PATERNOSTER ROW.
LONDON, E.C.4.
Printed in Great Britain.

'Silver Bells of Memory', a song by Harry Dale (Dale Collection)

travel 'upon the sea' either in the Royal Navy or merchant marine, in the army, or travelling to and fro within the expanding empire. As far as I can ascertain this song was written around 1880 in England and was then published a year later in the USA by Spear and Dehnhoff of New York, but as a piano arrangement by 'Thomas Maxwell', who was given the credit rather than Harry Dale.

'Silver Bells of Memory', by contrast, is more melancholic with reflections on happy times past at the close of another day. The first verse sets the tone:

> In the hush of eventide
> Sitting by my cottage door,
> Fancy softly seems to glide
> Backwards to the days of yore.
> And I hear in changeful swells
> Sweetest tones of melody,
> 'Tis the sound of silver bells,
> Silver bells of memory.'

The second verse recalls the passing of loved ones:

> Many faces have grown old,
> Many forms been laid to rest
> Underneath the churchyard mould.
> Ones I loved the most and best.
> Since I've heard the distant swells,
> Floating on the winds to me,
> Low and sweet the silver bells,
> Silver bells of memory.

At a time of high infant mortality, many deaths through disease and malnutrition, and loved ones departing for distant lands this would have had much appeal. There is evidence that it was written about 1876, and it appears in *American Sheet Music 1870–1885* published in Boston, USA, with his own name given credit as writer and composer. A version of this song was still being published in 1932 by Pitman-Hart in London, so it stood the test of time, but I have no idea who got the royalties, if any!

In contrast, I know he wrote some risqué songs which probably appealed more to male audiences. There are two songs where the complete words have survived entitled 'Alone I Did It' and 'Squeeze My Little Finger', the titles of which leave little to the modern imagination; the latter was, apparently, frequently sung by another music-hall favourite, George Ripon.

The opening verse of 'Squeeze My Little Finger' is almost philosophical, but the chorus that follows lowers the tone:

> This world's made up of sweet and sours,
>   not always shared out equal,
> Another gets what should be ours, then grumbling
>   is the sequel.
> In luck, all the rest of it, in war, in trade, in sporting,
> Imagine you've the best of it, especially in courting.
>
> Skip the gutter tra la la, Tottie do you love me,
> Ting ting au revoir, girls there's none above me.
> If you like me tell me so, do not let me linger,
> Tottie, if you love me, squeeze my little finger.

A couple of his other songs that have survived have lines that seem familiar, which makes me wonder if more modern songs may have been influenced by his original rhyming words. The first is entitled 'Pretty Little Sally' where the chorus is:

> Sally, Sally, pretty little Sally
> Sally down the alley
> Is pretty as could be.
> I'd like to marry Sally,
> Sweet Sally down the alley,
> But Sally down the alley
> She wouldn't marry me.

I am reminded of the Gracie Fields favourite 'Sally in Our Alley' where the chorus is:

> Sally, Sally, pride of our alley,
> Sally, Sally, don't ever wander
> Away from the alley and me …

'Does Thy Heart Beat True to Me', a song by Harry Dale
(Bodleian Library, University of Oxford)

In Harry Dale's song, 'In Praise of the Ladies', composed in the early 1880s, he writes:

> I'll sing in praise of the ladies fair,
> A very good theme you're well aware,
> Without them how very bad we'd fare.
> They comfort our homes and soothe our cares,
> And all the trouble of life they share.
> The dark, the fair, with curly hair,
> **The large, the small, the short, the tall,**
> **Oh bless their hearts I love them all.**
> With their rosy cheeks and dimpled chins;
> Their dress improvers that make you grin,
> But their pretty face your hearts will win
> And being in love will make you sing.

I have highlighted two of the lines that emerge in a similar format in the song that was probably the most popular army song of the Second World War namely: 'Bless 'em All', reputedly written by Fred Godfrey in 1917, but not sung with gusto until 1939 onwards. The first two lines of the chorus seem slightly familiar!

> Bless 'em all, Bless 'em all,
> The long and the short and the tall ...

For a man of minimum apparent education, writing and composing songs was a major achievement. Harry Dale knew his audience and what they liked and disliked. Versatile, topical, clever, funny, sad, romantic, shocking, local, national, I think his song writing palette embraced all of these features and the press time and time again comments that he delivered these songs in a fine baritone voice.

THE EIGHTIES AND CIRCUS DAYS

From the start of 1880 Harry Dale continued on the music-hall circuit but his billing now was more varied. For example, at the Alhambra Theatre in Belfast in March he was 'an admirable vocalist', at Templeton's Varieties in Halifax in June he was described as 'The Royal Court Jester', while in Bradford in August at the Star Music Hall he was 'The Musical Jester'. In August a visit to the Birmingham Concert Hall resulted in the comment 'a skilful performer on various instruments' whilst a rare foray into Wales saw him in Caernarvon in October at the Grand Pavilion. In the autumn he moved north of the border again with visits to MacFarland's Music Hall in Aberdeen where he was merely a 'comic vocalist', while in the Operetta House in Dundee he was an 'instrumental entertainer' and a welcome return to the Britannia in Glasgow in early December gave him three weeks of engagement as a 'talented musical entertainer'; before he moved to Leeds at Christmas and the Princess's Palace, where he shared top billing as the 'Court Jester' with Dan Leno, a very popular north of England comedian and clog dancer. It may be that he was adapting his act to suit the audiences, most of which he would know quite well, taking into account the differences in attitudes north and south of the border.

At this stage in his career he seems to have put some more thought into his future and the result was a careful and gradual change of direction. It is unlikely the decisions he took were made lightly, or without a great deal of consideration over a period of several months. For some twelve years he had been treading the boards of music halls throughout the British Isles and basically performing the same type of act utilising his musical skill and comic ability. But the music-hall scene was now very crowded with more and more performers appearing – of all ages and backgrounds – and the trick, as he would know, was to find a magic ingredient that distinguished him from that vast array. In modern 'management

Britannia Panopticon Music Hall building, Trongate, Glasgow 2007.
(Dale Collection)

speak', he was looking for USP – a Unique Selling Point. Some evidence of this gradual change appeared in 1880 when he advertised in *The Era* on 28 March:

> 'In Costly Raiment Clad' – N.P. Williams
> Alhambra, Belfast. Mr Harry Dale,
> The New Musical Court Jester
>
> Elaborate dresses; beautiful musical melange; smart & witty sayings; finely written and delivered lyrical speeches; songs unexcelled; voice, none better in the profession; at liberty for circuses during July & August. Terms, 'big', entertainment 'ditto'.
>
> Success still follows him – Addison. 'So get the start of the majestic world and bear the palm alone – Shakespeare.'

This remarkable advertisement brings together all his evolved talents and broadcasts his determination to exploit them not only on the music-hall stage, but now also in the circus arena.

The word 'jester' is defined as 'one who jests, a reciter, a buffoon, a court fool' and the jester has featured in English history since medieval times. Most of the kings and queens of England had a jester at court to entertain them. They were not always popular with their guests, however, as jesters were allowed a lot of freedom in their comments and songs that were designed primarily to amuse the sovereign.

It is now generally accepted that an Englishman, Philip Astley, was the founder of the circus that we know today. It bore no resemblance to the Roman spectacle where blood and gore seemed to be a key requirement, but the two did have the common purpose of entertaining the masses. Astley's circus was established at the end of the 18th century in London at a location called 'The Amphitheatre' near Waterloo Bridge. Astley had been a cavalry man in the army so his skill in riding horses and executing equestrian tricks formed the basis of his early circus shows. Within a few years he extended the programme to include acrobats, musical turns, jugglers, wire walkers and, of course, clowns and jesters. This formula was very popular and other circus proprietors emerged in the early 19th century such as Hengler, Bannister, the Cooke family and the famous Sanger brothers, George and John. The Astley circus had a fixed location, but the Sangers, for example, developed tented circuses that moved around the country and attracted audiences from rural as well as urban areas. By the mid- to late-nineteenth century there were numerous circuses, both permanent and tenting, throughout Britain and Ireland.

When Harry Dale published his advert there was extant a very well known and loved Victorian jester named William Wallett. He was born in Hull about 1813 and performed as a clown on the music hall stage and in several circuses. Following a command performance in 1844 before Queen Victoria and Albert, the Prince Consort, he was introduced to the Queen, and thereafter adopted the unofficial title of 'Queen's Jester'. This opportunistic piece of self-marketing ensured his career thereafter would be very successful, not just in Britain, but also across the United States which he visited several times. Latterly he lived in Beeston in Nottinghamshire where he died in 1892 aged 79 performing almost until the end of his life.

It seems to me that William Wallett was the model used by Harry Dale to shape his own future. Being a jester required much more than comic ability; the jester had to relate to the audience and entertain them, but be different in certain ways from the established clowns, grotesques and burlesques. He needed to have the ability to ad lib, be funny, be serious, be cultured and have charisma. By the end of his career, Harry Dale had been awarded several titles such as 'Court Jester', 'Lyrical Jester', 'Musical Jester', 'Prince of Jesters' and 'Shakespearean Jester' all of which reflected his multifaceted talents. I have no doubt he revelled in them all!

As well as changing direction he also seems to have developed new musical abilities. In later reports of his act in 1880 and 1881, mention is made of his performances with musical bells, musical glasses, the cornet, English concertina and other instruments supplementing his established baritone voice. It is difficult not to admire the time and effort he must have put in to develop these additional skills.

To emphasise the change in direction he had adopted, he had a studio photograph taken of himself dressed in 'cap and bells' and that captures a man at the pinnacle of his career. The black and white photograph does not show the colours of his 'elaborate dresses' but his stance shows a certain arrogance as he looks straight at the camera. I do not know how tall he was, but most of my male Dale family have been between 5'2" and 5'8" so I am sure he would be somewhere in that range. He would be roughly 36 when he posed for the photograph. The moustache with its drooping ends was a common feature of Victorian men's faces, but his eyes seem a little distant to me. The shape and length of his nose I recognise as a 'Dale nose', as it appears in later generations. As I never met him and do not know anyone who did, there is no record as to his demeanour, his behaviour, his philosophy of life in general, and importantly, his attitude to others. (See p.8).

His success on the stage and in the circus arena clearly stemmed from steely determination backed by hard work in developing his craft. Perhaps this determination overflowed into his private life where I suspect he was a hard task-master. I think he was also a dedicated teacher as the sons and daughters of his family who became entertainers themselves were well taught in musical skills and carved out their own careers in due course.

His song entitled 'Silver Bells of Memory' mentioned in the last chapter was advertised in *The Graphic* at the end of October 1880 as being 'post free for 18 stamps'. I have no idea how many copies he sold but this particular song 'arranged for the pianoforte by George West' was still being published and sold fifty years later as 'Written & Composed by Harry Dale'. I am sure he did not rely on the income from his compositions to survive, but they would be a useful financial supplement and were a form of advertising for him.

Inevitably, when he was doing well, an advertisement appeared in *The Era*. This one is dated 21 November 1880.

Harry Dale, the Celebrated Versatile Artiste, the Comic Vocalist, the Renowned Baritone, the Court Jester.

A nine-line summary of an entry in the *Dundee Telegraph* then followed praising all aspects of his performance which concluded: 'Offers from Principal Circuses for Summer Season invited. Address H. Dale, Imperial Court Jester'. He was aiming high as the phrase 'Principal Circuses' obviously excluded the smaller, less attractive establishments that were now in existence.

His family continued to increase and during December 1880, he and his wife, Sarah Ann, had a fourth son named Stanley Henry Dale in Manchester, where they lived at Ridgeway Street.

The variety of acts alongside Harry Dale at the northern provincial music halls was quite astonishing. Many were household names amongst the Victorian audiences, whilst others were soon forgotten. Examples of both who shared a bill with Harry Dale in the 1880/81 seasons included 'the great Scotch athletes Donald Dinnie and George Davidson'; Nellie Leybourne, Flora Etheridge, serio-comic; Vern & Volt, the 'breakneck two'; Madame Milano's Ballet Troupe; George Hall, the 'Australian Samson'; the Lupino family; Orville Parker, banjo soloist and stump orator; Oscar Leroy, wire walker; Dermot & Doyle, Irish entertainers' and so on.

The year 1881 was a census year with the Dale family domiciled in Manchester at Ridgeway Street, so the household on census day – 4 April – showed:

Henry Thomas Dale, Married, Age 36,
    Vocalist Musician, born Birmingham
Ada Dale, Wife, Age 29, born Liverpool
Amy Dale, Daughter, Age 9, Scholar, born London,
    Middlesex
Albert Dale, Son, Age 8, Scholar, born Oldham, Lancs

Harry Dale, Son, Age 6, Scholar, born Oldham, Lancs.
Ernest Dale, Son, Age 4, Scholar, born Manchester, Lancs.
Ella Dale, Daughter, Age 2, born Manchester, Lancs.
Stanley Dale, Son, Age 5 months, born Manchester, Lancs.

The only error was the birthplace of Ella Dale, which was actually Sunderland in County Durham, and not Manchester. An understandable error in view of the family travels around the country. The correct birthplace for her appeared in subsequent census details. A close search of the 1881 census also revealed the presence of Harry Dale's mother, Mary Ann Corrock, now aged 62, who was living at Worseley Street, Manchester with her third husband, John Corrock. This address was within walking distance of Ridgeway Street. John Corrock was a tailor to trade, the son of a 'robe maker', and I have often wondered if he was responsible for making the ornate and elaborate jester costumes for his son-in-law.

The rest of 1881 saw Harry at a variety of music halls, many now distant memories, such as the 'Gaiety Temperance Theatre' in Preston, the 'Star Music Hall' in Carlisle, the Macclesfield 'Circus of Varieties' and the 'Alhambra' in Sheffield.

This last hall was the locus of Harry Dale's first attempt at management. He had been performing in Edinburgh for a couple of weeks in April 1882 at 'Moss's Varieties', a forerunner of H.E. Moss' huge variety theatre empire. He moved from Edinburgh to the Alhambra in late April as manager where the proprietor of this relatively modern establishment was Mr W. Cooper. A report in *The Era* describes the complete destruction of the theatre by fire – a hazard of all gas-lit Victorian music halls – on Thursday 1 June 1882. Fortunately the fire took hold sometime in the early morning and there was no loss of life. Clearly, performers booked had lost their contracts, including Harry Dale. His response was rapid and unusual. In an advert in *The Era* of 29 July he let it be known 'until the rebuilding of the Alhambra I have taken the Sawmill Tavern, Matilda Street, Sheffield. Music Saturday, Sunday and Monday Evenings'. A future love affair with licensed premises seems to have originated here.

Although I have traced his performances week by week during 1880 and 1881 it was only in 1882 that I think he made his first appearance in the circus ring. In the *Blackpool Times* write-up of August 1901, referred to previously, he mentions the well known circus entrepreneur James Newsome as providing him with 'an excellent engagement at his circus in Preston'. In September 1882 Harry Dale performed at the New Gaiety Palace Theatre in Preston where he was given a good report as a clown and jester. Shortly thereafter, Newsome's Circus opened in Preston in October at the Hippodrome and one of the many acts was 'a musical melange by Harry Dale, one of the clowns'. I can only conjecture, but I am sure James Newsome and Harry Dale must have met in Preston that autumn, and he was offered the chance to perform in the ring. It would be quite a different environment from the music-hall stage as his audience was now surrounding him rather than in front. The sound in a circular arena would be different and he would need good collaboration with the circus orchestra to achieve continuity. All the evidence shows he liked this challenging situation and he moved more and more into the circus arena as he got older, eventually abandoning the music-hall stage altogether. There was also the advantage that the circus tended to perform in the same place for several weeks during the season, so there was the chance of some stability in his life compared to his music hall existence where a different location every couple of weeks precluded this.

In the *Blackpool Times* article, Harry Dale comments that after his Preston appearance, he 'qualified himself as a jester and as such appeared with Charlie Keith's circus in Bradford'. I am not clear what he meant by 'qualify' as during November and December 1882 he was performing in the music hall at Hull; the Alhambra Palace Theatre, Great Grimsby; at the Corporation Concert Hall, then the New Hall of Varieties at Gateshead for two weeks. Nowadays, if we read the word 'qualification', we anticipate some sort of apprenticeship with relevant examinations to follow but I suspect this was not the case. No doubt he polished up his musical talents and kept abreast of local news as the jester could, and would, make fun of local situations to the delight of the audience. Charles Keith's Circus opened in Bradford in December 1882 and a report in *The Era* for 6 January 1883 states: 'Harry Dale, the lyrical clown is an addition ... and deserving of the best support of the public.'

For the rest of that year he flitted between the music-hall stage and the odd circus appearance. Another child was born to him and Sarah Ann on 29 April 1883 at Ecclesall Bierlow, Sheffield and was named Lottie Dale. She was the third daughter and I noted Henry Thomas continued to describe himself as a 'file-cutter' on the birth certificate although he had been in show business by this time for some 15 continuous years.

Virtually all his performances now were in the north of England, Scotland and Ireland. The whole of Ireland was still an integral part of Great Britain and when he was across the Irish Sea, he appeared in Belfast, Dublin, Cork and all over the island. It was probably more economical to remain there for a few weeks rather than return to England, where he lived, at the end of every couple of weeks. By the autumn of 1884 he was in contact with one of the great circus entrepreneurs of the time, Edinburgh-based John Henry Cooke. I noted he was performing as, 'Harry Dale, the well-known musical jester' with Cooke's Circus in Greenock, to the west of Glasgow, during October of that year. He then moved north to Aberdeen in December, appearing in Cooke's Circus in the Granite City and the *Aberdeen Free Press* of 16 December reported 'Mr Harry Dale made his first appearance as a musical jester of good accomplishments.'

On 15 December 1884 Sarah Ann Dale gave birth to another daughter in Ecclesall Bierlow. She was named Frances Leah Dale but she died in June 1885 in Prestwich, near Manchester. Harry Dale could not have been present at the birth as he was in Aberdeen and it is possible he was not present when the baby died. This was a tragedy for the family, but Sarah Ann gave birth to 11 children, and this was the only one lost in infancy.

During 1885 Harry moved across the country as usual with appearances in the Circus Hall, Doncaster in May, for example, followed by June and July at Harmston's Circus, performing in Ginnett's Circus building in Derby, where 'the fun was kept going by Harry Dale, Matthewson and the Brothers de Vere'.

He was back in Market Street, Aberdeen with Cooke in November and the *Aberdeen Free Press* praised him on the 10 November 1885 as 'a musical entertainer of considerable merit'. *The Northern Figaro* also carried a series of commentaries about Cooke's Circus with some emphasis on the talents of clowns such as James Hayes, Little Pickles and 'Mr Harry Dale, a witty jester'. When Christmas arrived, John Henry Cooke, as was his established habit, put on a pantomime. Cooke himself was a renowned and skilled equestrian performer and had a great love for the horse, so many of his annual pantomimes were themed accordingly. No exception was made in 1885 when the pantomime was 'Ride a Cock Horse to

Banbury Cross' which an advertisement in the *Northern Figaro* on 26 December indicated was written and arranged by Mr Harry Dale. New and incidental music was composed and arranged by Mr G. Spencer with 'magnificent and appropriate dresses designed by Mrs J.H. Cooke and Mrs J. Middleton and executed by numerous assistants'. To exploit this marketable situation, Cooke put on two daily performances during the Christmas and New Year holidays, the doors opening at 2 p.m. and 7 p.m. On New Year's Day, there were three performances with doors opening at 11.30 a.m., 2 p.m. and 7 p.m. The most expensive reserved seats were three shillings each, whilst the cheapest, in the Gallery, were sixpence each. (See p.48).

The *Aberdeen Free Press* reported on the 26 December 1885 that Harry Dale's writing and arrangement of the pantomime 'does him credit, as numerous bits, local and other, find a place in the programme and they are not without pith and point'. *The Northern Figaro* also reiterates praise for Harry Dale's writing and in addition commends him for the part he played in the production – Mother Goose (his first appearance as a cross dresser as far as I know). Cooke's Circus completed its season in Aberdeen in early 1886 with a major benefit for Harry Dale and 'not withstanding the inclemency of the weather, he had a bumper house' reported the *Aberdeen Weekly Journal*. Generously, he alluded to the courtesy of John Henry Cooke and the attentions of the press.

From Aberdeen he moved to Ginnett's Circus in Belfast then Dublin finishing in late March before returning to England and a season with Rowland's New York Circus in Croydon in April. Rowland's and Harry Dale then crossed the English Channel to Jersey in July and amongst the lesser artists taking part was a young lady named Miss Amy Dale. I am sure this was his eldest daughter, born in 1872, and therefore 14 years old, but it is not clear from the programme what she was doing although latterly she was known as a fine singer and pianist.

Now labelled 'The Prince of Jesters', Harry Dale returned to Cooke's Circus in Greenock in late Augus, then moved to Edinburgh in November.

The highlight for John Henry Cooke was undoubtedly the opening of his new permanent Royal Circus in East Fountain-bridge, Edinburgh in November 1886. Cooke lived in Edinburgh and managed his circus business from there although his circus was found throughout the UK. I have noted it in Birmingham, Doncaster, Bradford and Manchester, for example, as well as established Scottish locations such as Dundee, Greenock, Perth, Glasgow, Dumfries and Aberdeen as well as Edinburgh.

My great grandfather was linked with John Henry Cooke for many years and it is worth mentioning that Harry Dale's sons and daughters were also performers with Cooke's Circus later on. I will illustrate this in later chapters. Perhaps nepotism crept into the relationship, but in fairness to Cooke, he was well known for setting a high standard, so any performer who fell below this would be unlikely to appear again.

The opening of Cooke's Circus on 19 November 1886 has been described in the first chapter of this book, and it was a great success. Harry Dale benefited in several ways as his performance as a jester and clown was noted, but his ability to write an amusing and appropriate pantomime was also praised. The pantomime performed in Aberdeen the year before was repeated in Edinburgh, a situation where geography assisted the managers and performers in the circus, and no doubt the same jokes, songs and clowning

London Museum Concert Hall, Digbeth, Birmingham 2008 (Dale Collection)

took place, a luxury not possible in the 21st century with radio, TV and the press being all-pervasive.

After Cooke's Circus completed its season in February 1887, Harry moved to Bristol with Sanger's Circus then Exeter with Rowland's in February. He was back in Jersey again with Rowland's second string in July while William Rowland's main circus was at the Crystal Palace in London. November saw him back in Edinburgh with John Henry Cooke's Circus where the audience could enjoy 'new local hits by Harry Dale'.

The year 1888 saw him in the spring with Ohmy's Circus in the north of England while a further season with Rowland's New York Circus commenced in Derby in June. He then had a brief interlude in management at the Tyne Music Hall in South Shields commencing in September. This hall was advertised as the 'largest in the north' and was leased by his old friend from Sunderland days, Stuart Henry Bell. The hall opened with a fanfare but at the interval part of the pit flooring gave way causing a brief period of panic amongst the audience. However, Harry Dale, as manager, went to the front of the stage, explained the situation and calmed the patrons who for the most part resumed their seats. In the best show business tradition, the show continued and the hall was repaired the next day.

In October 1888 he was back in the arena with the Grand Circus in Manchester, operated by Weston Gibbs. It then moved to Warrington, concluding in March 1889. A public spat between Gibbs and Dale took place on the last evening which was reported in the local papers, although the bulk of the audience thought it was part of the show!

On 29 January 1889 the fifth girl in the family was born at 18 Wellington Street, Bradford in Manchester, Lancashire – not Bradford in Yorkshire – and was named Vera Maud Dale. The birth certificate shows the occupation of Henry Thomas Dale as a 'musician'. He had obviously decided, at last, to drop his previous occupational description of 'file-cutter.' She was the ninth child in the family and by this time sufficient accommodation for the Dales must have been quite difficult to find. It emerged that towards the beginning of the year Harry Dale had become the proprietor of a small hotel in Sankey Street, Warrington, named 'The Millstone'. He seems to have operated a small music hall in the premises, honing his managerial skills, and providing his long-suffering wife

The Northern Figaro.

JOHN HENRY COOKE'S

ROYAL CIRCUS,

MARKET STREET, ABERDEEN.

———o———

PRODUCTION ON

SATURDAY, 26th DECEMBER, 1885,

And at every Performance until further notice, of JOHN
HENRY COOKE'S GRAND EQUESTRIAN PANTOMIME,

RIDE A COCK HORSE

TO

BANBURY CROSS

On a scale of Magnificence and Grandeur, and with every
attention to completeness and detail, seldom (if ever) attempted
in a Circus.

———o———

Written and Arranged by

Mr. HARRY DALE.

New and Incidental Music, Composed and Arranged by
Mr. G. SPENCER.
The Magnificent and Appropriate Dresses Designed by Mrs.
J. H. COOKE and Mrs. J. MIDDLETON, and executed
by numerous Assistants.
New Scenery by Mr. GEORGE STEPHENS.
The Properties, Masks, and General Paraphernalia by
Mr. LYTTON.
The Whole Produced under the Personal Superintendence of

Mr. JOHN HENRY COOKE.

———o———

Notice about Cooke's Circus pantomime *Ride a Cock Horse* in Aberdeen, 1885
(Dale Collection)

with a period of stability. He advertised the hotel under the
'Professional Apartments' column of *The Era* ('Three Lines a
Shilling') in August claiming 'the most comfortable and only
professional house of call in Warrington' with the proprietor 'Harry
Dale, Prince of Jesters. Space for others, harmony every evening'.

In September 1889 he was to be found at Elphinstone's Circus
in Huddersfield for a couple of weeks which he followed with a
quick October visit to Rowland's New York Circus in West
Hartlepool. The Britannia Music Hall in Glasgow beckoned him
back again at the end of that month for a week where 'Harry Dale
is a capital jester', then he moved south across the border again to
Sheffield during November at the Grand Circus.

Showman that he was, he advertised in *The Era* again in early
November quoting from the *Huddersfield Examiner* of 11 October:
'Harry Dale makes an admirable jester and … is a fine elocutionist
and recites with good dramatic effect'. To use modern management
speak: If you've got it, flaunt it!

He returned to Glasgow in December and was able to dust
down his pantomime yet again as he appeared with Transfield's
Circus at its new location in Ingram Street. 'Ride a Cock Horse to
Banbury Cross' was a great success with the *Glasgow Evening Times*
of 30 December 1889 which commented 'the story written and
arranged by Mr Harry Dale, does him credit'; and he also took the
part of Mother Goose to some acclaim. The circus was in action
through the New Year finishing some time in early February 1890.

This decade of his career was busy and successful and he must
have had an iron constitution to cope with the travel, the differing
accommodation and the variety of food. Being on the road for long
periods required good health and he seems to have been fortunate
in that aspect of his life.

THE NINETIES AND OVERSEAS VISITS

The start of 1890 saw Harry Dale in Glasgow performing at Transfield's Circus in Glasgow. An advertisement in *The Glasgow Herald* and the *Glasgow Evening Times* extolled:

Grand Holiday Production
'Ride a Cock Horse to Banbury Cross' by HARRY DALE characters by Harry Hemphrey, W. Coster, Madam Armstrong, Miss Edie, Funny Mathewson, The Leonards, Harry Dale. The entire company and 100 extra artistes with four daily performances during the holiday period.

I have no doubt that this was the same version of 'Ride a Cock Horse' that Harry Dale wrote and performed in for John Henry Cooke four years earlier. The Glasgow audiences were unlikely to have seen the Edinburgh based circus, and with four years in between he was quite safe in pulling it out of the drawer for another airing. However, four performances a day was hard graft for all the performers as well as the horses and other animals involved.

Transfield's Circus finished its season sometime in early February but Harry Dale is found in January in Cork, then in Belfast in late February performing with Ginnett's Circus. *The Belfast News-Letter* reports the circus located at Glengall Place in the city: 'the circus opened on Monday with a long and attractive programme. Artists appearing were the Brothers De Courcy, Madame Pauline, Harry Dale and Louie & Elba …'

The Ginnett family was another famous circus dynasty founded by Jean Pierre Ginnett, a French cuirassier captured at the Battle of Waterloo in 1815 but who chose to remain in England after his release. His own circus was established by the 1850s and after his death in 1861 members of his family carried on the business.

From February through to late March Harry Dale remained in the Irish city, which was a hive of industrial activity at that period, and a good market for the ever popular circus. During April he returned to Warrington where he now took up residence and re-launched himself with another new venture. He took custody of a public house in Horsemarket Street, near the centre of the town, called the Hop Pole and renamed it the 'Hop Pole Concert Hall.' He created a small music hall where there were already two large theatres: the Theatre Royal for drama, and the Empire Theatre for variety. The only marginal competition was another public house offering musical entertainment named the 'White Bull'. With his extensive contacts and 20 years of experience in the business, he promoted weekly entertainment bills for almost a 12 month period. His patient wife, Sarah Ann, and his growing family lived above the pub for the duration. I was delighted, during a visit to Warrington in 2006, to find the pub still in place showing all its Victorian elegance on the outside. The interior had been upgraded and the concert hall itself seems to have disappeared under new buildings. I suspect the size of the audience was modest.

The first *Era* report was on 5 April 1890 when the artists on duty were Ben Talbot, comic; Miss Lily Le Breton; Miss Jessie Lamont, serio-comic; Master H. Dale, solo cornettist; and Miss A. Dale contralto vocalist, as well as 'the popular Harry Dale himself'. This entry signals the appearance of two of his talented children, Harry Dale, his second son aged 15 and his eldest daughter, Amy Dale,

Hop Pole Public House, Warrington. 2008. (Dale Collection)

who would have been 18 years old at the time. Subsequent entries in *The Era* reveal Amy was a popular singer and Harry senior seems to have used this venture as a means of introducing not only her and her brother to the stage and a live audience, but also, gradually, other members of his family.

The Era reveals that Harry Dale had a pool of regular performers who rotated each week or fortnight giving him a variety of male and female comics, singers, dancers, illusionists and conjurors. The local reporter was generous in his praise with comments such as: 'a pleasing entertainment', 'business is unusually brisk', 'entertainment supplied by the popular proprietor is greatly appreciated' and so on. The most frequent performers included Albert West, a comic; Rose Verdant, a sentimental soprano; Maud Neilson, a serio-comic; Walter Gilmore, a character vocalist; Ethel Shannon, the English flower girl; and of course, Amy Dale, contralto. Harry supplemented this core of performers with an exotic or two each week such as Miss Bertie Brandon, male impersonator; Monsieur & Madame Diamond, knife throwers; Harry Sungham, Negro artist; Madame Gourlay, whistler and ballet vocalist; and Peter Brodie, Ethiopian burlesque comedian – whatever that means.

The *Liverpool Mercury* of September 1890 reported on the licence applications and renewals in Warrington. The Chief Constable said the applicant for the Hop Pole, Mr Harry Dale, had only recently become the owner. The former owner had been fined and the premises had a bad reputation but the police had no fault to find with Mr Dale. The licence was renewed.

The final relevant entry in *The Era* is dated 7 March 1891 and states: 'Warrington, Hop Pole Concert Hall: With the present week the popular Harry closes his connection with this hall. Newcomers are Walter Gilmore, vocal comedian, Maud Neilson, serio-comic and Mr Dale also works a pleasing turn.' The hall was taken over by a Mr J. Coop who re-named it 'Coop's Varieties' and carried on the music-hall entertainment.

In the process of running the concert hall, his wife, Sarah Ann, gave birth on 20 December 1890 to their fifth son, Sydney Edgar Dale. Interestingly, the birth certificate shows Harry Dale, the father, as a 'licensed victualler'. Living above the pub with its noisy nightly entertainment must have been difficult for his wife and in these days giving birth at home was very much the norm. Young

Sydney Edgar had the sound of music in his ears from day one so it is not surprising that in later life he also became a professional musician. On 6 April 1891 the census was taken and I was surprised to find that the family had left Warrington and moved to Stockport in Cheshire where they were now domiciled at 69 Lower Hillgate. This was the address of an establishment called the Victoria Hotel so Harry Dale seems to have acquired a taste for operating licensed premises. Stockport at that time boasted a drama theatre called the New Theatre Royal.

The Victoria Hotel was much larger than the Hop Pole, and had an interesting history. Originally called the Jolly Hatters the establishment in the early 1840s had a long room added by the landlord, Mr George Bramwell, which was fitted with seats and a stage, and some dressing room facilities. The name was changed to the Victoria Hotel and acquired a reputation as a 'singing pub'. The premises closed in 1956 and the building was eventually demolished. I think its reputation as a singing establishment was the attraction to Harry Dale.

Unfortunately, I have been unable to discover what Harry achieved here. There is no reference to him or the hotel in published papers I have consulted except for the census entry. I found that later in 1891 he was back with the touring circuses again, in particular with Julian's Tenting Circus so the venture at the hotel does not seem to have been a success. Further evidence shows he returned to live in Warrington in late 1891 and stayed there for the rest of his life.

The 1891 census entry for the Dale family showed:

Henry T. Dale, Married, Age 46, professional vocalist,
    born Birmingham
Sarah A. Dale, Wife, Age 40, born Liverpool
Amy M.A. Dale, Daughter, Age 19, Unm, professional
    pianist, born London
Albert Dale, Son, Age 18, Unm. bar tender, born Oldham,
    Lancs.
Harry Dale, Son, Age 16, Unm. bar tender, born Oldham,
    Lancs.
Ella Dale, Daughter, Age 12, Unm, b. Sunderland,
    Co Durham.
Ernest Dale, Son, Age 14, Unm. Born Manchester

Stanley Dale, Son, Age 10, Unm. Born Manchester
Lottie Dale, Daughter, Age 7, born Sheffield.
Vera Maud Dale, daughter, Age 2, born Manchester
Sydney Edgar Dale, Son, Age 3 months, born Warrington

Both Albert and Harry Dale, his sons, were described as 'bar
tenders' which was very likely as they lived in licensed premises, but
Amy Dale was not described as a 'vocalist' after her performances at
the Hop Pole, but as a 'professional pianist'.

Harry Dale's employment with Julian's Tented Circus saw him
back in the arena as the Jester. John Julian, real name Woodrow, was
originally a clown and set up his circus about 1889. He initially
concentrated on the north of England, but in 1891 he toured in the
south west visiting Devises, Taunton, Redruth and Plymouth. His
circus closed down sometime in the late 1890s.

Towards the end of 1891 Harry Dale appeared with Widdowson
& Grafton's Circus in Wigan, then Culeen's Circus in Rochdale,
and he followed these with a season in Rowland's New York Circus
in Wolverhampton which had 'returned to the scene of former
triumphs'.

He returned to Widdowson & Grafton in February 1892 when
they entertained in Lincoln and in the summer months he was to
be found in Southport with Quinnette's Circus, Blyth in
Northumberland with Tudor's, and in November with Wulff's
Continental Circus in London where he was billed as the Ring
Master.

Edward Wulff was another popular circus proprietor of the day.
He had a great love of the horse and spectacular equestrian acts were
some of the attractions he offered to his patrons. He often operated
on the Continent but tended to return to London in the winter
months. Harry Dale was obviously well regarded by Edward Wulff
if he had such an important role as Ring Master.

Entering 1893 the published entries for Harry Dale's activities
throughout the British Isles suddenly ceased in both *The Era* and
The Stage. This puzzle was solved by an advert in *The Era* dated 17
February 1894 which states:

Mr Harry Dale
The Great Talking & Singing Jester arrived in England per
SS *Goorkha*, February 7th

> After more than a year with Harmston's Great Circus in the Far East – Hong-Kong, Phillipines, Straits Settlements, Sumatra, Java, India etc with usual success.
>
> Press Notice of last but one town, *Rangoon Times* December 1st 1893
>
> Mr Harry Dale, the jester. His playing on the English concertina is a thing to astonish everyone, and his elocution is splendid.
>
> At Liberty, Short or Long Engagements, Tenting or otherwise
>
> Address: 10 Orford Avenue, Warrington.

Strangely, the passenger list for the SS *Goorkha* sailing from Calcutta to London does not record a 'Harry Dale', but does show a 'John Dale', aged 36, an actor. By early 1894, Harry Dale was 49, so for some reason he was travelling incognito.

Whilst Harry was on this long tour, Sarah Ann gave birth on 26 July 1893 to their last child, another girl, named Doris May. Sarah Ann was now almost 43 so it was perhaps a relief for her that with 10 surviving children from 11 births, the family was now complete. A pleasant surprise for her husband when he returned from his travels to find a six month old baby demanding his attention. I am puzzled how his large family managed to survive whilst he was away with Harmston's Circus. Some arrangement must have been made to provide Sarah Ann with money for the rent, food, clothes and so on, but I have no knowledge of how this was done.

What was not mentioned in the above advert was the death at 49 of William Harmston in Singapore from dysentery and complications. His widow continued to run the circus after this sudden death, then their son, William junior, took over until the mid 1930s.

I am impressed at the survival rate amongst the performers on these Far East tours, considereing all the tropical fevers, diseases and illnesses for which there was no treatment. Harry Dale soldiered on but at 50, I think he was inclining more towards the managerial side of the circus.

This appeared in *The Era* dated 22 September 1894:

> WANTED – the Circus world to know that Mr Harry Dale, Prince of Jesters, Musical Vocal & Talking, is still with Lord George Sanger, engaged especially as Ringmaster, also with

the following: Herr Wulff, Claude Ginnett, Rowlands, Harmistons, Throughout China, Netherlands, Java, Sumatra, Acheen, Straits Settlements India etc. The most resonant voice in the business, can write, compose and arrange pantomimes and equestrian spectacles. Can give a good musical act. Offers invited: 10 Orford Avenue, Warrington.

Self-promotion was a strong element in Harry Dale's character, and he was an inveterate name-dropper. The most well known of these names to circus audiences was 'Lord' George Sanger.

'Lord' George Sanger was possibly the leading circus proprietor of the Victorian era. Born about 1827 in Newbury, Berkshire, he and his brothers John and William started in the circus business about 1848 in a small way, building their reputation on the variety of acts they presented and the size of both the permanent facilities and the tented shows. George and John decided to go their separate ways so George headed for the Continent initially while John concentrated on Britain. George returned in due course, founding the Showman's Guild of which he was President until 1909. He met a sad end, however, being murdered in 1911 by one of his employees. His brother, 'Lord' John Sanger had died in 1889 in Margate and was equally famous as a circus proprietor. After he died, the circus that bore his name continued under the management of his sons well into the 1930s.

As ringmaster, Harry Dale would have plenty opportunity to show off his resonant voice, good diction and sense of humour. The circus moved to Cambridge in November 1894 then had its 46th season in London starting on 3 December.

There is an interesting comment in *The Era* of 2 February 1895 when Harry was performing at Quaglieni's Circus. The report states: 'Mr Harry Dale, the well known author and jester on whom the mantle of the late W.F. Wallett seems to have fallen, is very successful as the jester.' William Wallett, the highly popular Queen's Jester, mentioned in Chapter 4, had died in 1892, aged 79.

On 9 June the Dale family celebrated the wedding of their first child, Amy Dale, who married Richard Bailey in St Paul's Church, Warrington. Amy, now aged 23, was a singer and pianist and her husband was described as an 'earthen ware dealer'.

Performances in 1895 throughout the country culminated in a

further season in December with the Grand Circus in Hanley where 'Apollo, the Scottish Hercules executes some marvellous feats and the horsemanship of Harry Boswell is well shown'. Harry Boswell was also the proprietor and director of this particular circus.

January 1896 saw Harry Dale in Croydon at the National Hall & Theatre of Varieties, 'a hall recently refurbished at a cost of £2000 by the proprietor, Mr Gardiner Hales,' while in February the same reviewer emphasised the 'masterly vocal powers of Harry Dale.' June saw Harry entertaining the Aberdonians who flocked to John Henry Cooke's Circus, and the *Aberdeen Weekly Journal* of 30 June praises Cooke's own performance on a thoroughbred American horse named 'Lexington' while his attractive daughter Ernestine Rosa Cooke exhibited 'a flight of trained pigeons'. One of Harry's contributions was 'an amusing speech on the new woman, followed by a recitation rendered in splendid style'. Just how did he define a new woman? We will never know. The season in Aberdeen finished in August and the circus moved south to Paisley until the end of October then opened for the season in Edinburgh in early November.

John Henry Cooke was very skilled at marketing his circus, putting on a major pantomime each year where the entire cast took a variety of parts. The press reports for December 1896 revealed the annual pantomime was 'Jack the Giant Killer' produced 'with a splendour and completeness never surpassed'. A 'first rate libretto has been provided with a number of fresh up-to-date songs by Harry Dale and with handsome properties and mechanical effects by Mr Henry Duckworth and beautiful dresses by Miss Amy Samwells'. It goes without saying that the circus was 'crowded to the doors with an appreciative audience'. Harry had the part of King Arthur, perhaps in keeping with his 52 years, but there seems no doubt he was a popular performer not just with the audience, but also his fellow professionals.

Finishing in Edinburgh sometime in February 1897, he remained with Cooke's Circus as it toured Scotland including a foray to Rothesay on the Isle of Bute, one of the leading resorts on the Clyde, at the height of the Glasgow Fair holiday season.

In August he was billed with Ohmy's Circus in Blackburn. Known as 'King' Ohmy, this popular proprietor was born in 1854 and his real name was Joseph Smith. He was a highly skilled trapeze and aerial performer who would plummet from a great height in the middle of his act, his apparently catastophic fall stopped inches above the patrons by sliding ropes round his ankles. It was said that so many of the frightened audience shouted 'Oh my' that he adopted it as his stage name! He established his own circus in the north of England, which toured for several years.

From Blackburn, the Cotton Town, in August Harry moved to Edward Paddock's Royal British Circus at Bootle in September then had a season with Zaro's Circus in Coventry from October until mid-December. James Zaro provided an interesting programme including the violinist Paganini Redivivus, Japanese dancers, Sharman's Troupe of Dogs, a trick bicycling act by the Lavender Troupe, and of course, Harry Dale, the lyrical jester.

Harry saw in the New Year of 1898 back with Transfield's Circus in Walsall. He stayed with Transfield's during the spring, appearing in Hyde, near Manchester, then moved to Stockport with the Imperial Circus in June, where the proprietor and manager was another well known Victorian gymnast and acrobat, Toney Felix. *The Stage* of 16 June reported the sketch 'Dick Turpin's Ride to York' was 'capitally performed by Messrs Cullen, Harry Dale and Toney Felix'.

Towards the end of 1898 and at the beginning of 1899, a series of adverts appeared in *The Era* for John Batty's Circus in Stockton on Tees, where the general manager was none other than Harry Dale. The adverts stated 'this is a first class circus, and pays first class salaries' which must have been quite an incentive for potential performers! This circus entertained the inhabitants of Stockton until March 1899 with such acts as Colibri's Midgets, Lockharts Elephants, Permane's Bears, Peter Simple, the clown, and another clown and auguste named Wamba. Nepotism had reared its head again but I am not sure which of his sons – Albert or Harry – who had adopted this specific stage name, this particular Wamba was.

At the end of the circus season, another advert appeared in *The Era* dated 22 April 1899, announcing the departure of Wirth's Australian Circus for an eight-month tour. Philip Wirth was the son of Johannes Wirth, a German national who went to Australia during the gold boom. The family had some success in Australia with their circus and Philip brought it to England about 1897. The 1899 departure was for South Africa and amongst the performers sailing on the SS *Braemar Castle* was Harry Dale, the Prince of

Jesters. His last tour round the Far East perhaps whetted his appetite to see more of the Empire. Wirth's timing was interesting as tension between the two Boer Republics – the Orange Free State and the Transvaal – and Britain, was mounting.

Wirth's Circus opened in Cape Town in May 'after an absence from the colony of some five years' to a big house. Artists performing included the Saxon Trio; Miss Adele Libra, slack wire equilibriste; Miss Tona Ginnett equestrienne; and Mr Harry Dale, labelled as 'the Queen's Jester'. From Cape Town the circus moved around the colony and the Boer Republics with visits to Ladysmith, Dundee, East London, Port Elizabeth, Pretoria, Johannesburg and Pietermaritzburg. War between the Boer Republics and Britain commenced on 11 October 1899 but by that time Wirth's Circus, curtailing its stay by seven weeks, had returned to Britain sailing in September from Cape Town when the military situation deteriorated.

The *Glasgow Herald* of 2 October 1899 carried an article about the situation in South Africa and amongst those interviewed returning from there was Harry Dale.

He said he had toured with Wirth's Circus and 'ten weeks ago when in Pretoria, he had visited President Kruger to ask his patronage for a performance at the circus'. The president responded that 'in the current situation he could not visit an English circus'. Mr Dale did not think much of the president but said the young Boers were itching for a fight encouraged by the older Boers who said 'the only British flag they saw was a white one'. This was a reference to the Battle of Majuba in 1881 when the Boers defeated a British army. Harry Dale's final comments criticised the high taxation exerted by the Boers on everything, 'except the air' and on his way home he had been robbed of thirteen guineas at Vereeniging. A patriot he was, and he made sure the world at large knew it!

Prematurely back in Britain, he had a vacant diary and immediately took out a large advert in *The Era* of 7 October quoting a number of South African newspaper comments on his performances. 'Keen witted and smart at repartee,' 'elocutionist of great ability' and 'clever in his recitations and can crack a good joke' are three examples. There was also a mention of a publication entitled *Book of Songs & Jokes of Harry Dale* that was handed out by him, and there was much interest in his songs in particular, where one

newspaper prophesised 'an epidemic of Dale music even after the
Circus has gone'.

I have been very fortunate to obtain a damaged copy from a
second cousin of mine of the very publication referred to, priced
one penny in pre-decimal money. It makes fascinating reading as
the words for a few of his most popular songs are provided and
there is an invitation to anyone interested in the actual music to
write to the appropriate publisher. The section containing his jokes
is missing, unfortunately.

He found employment to fill his diary towards the end of 1899
with appearances in the circus in Stockton on Tees and in
December he was back in South Shields with Algie's Circus. The
nineteenth century closed – a relatively satisfying period for him –
and the twentieth century beckoned, but there were storm clouds
on the horizon as new technology crept into the entertainment
business: it was called the biograph, or film.

THE NEW CENTURY

The dawn of the 20th century saw Harry Dale performing in South Shields, near the mouth of the River Tyne, with Algie's New Grand Circus. A move to Stockton on Tees in April saw him with Batty's Circus, then a return to Algie's in the June had him on the same bill as the Sisters Sullivan, top boot dancers; James Mackenzie, Highland dancer; and the equestrian performers St John Pinder and Miss Bell, amongst others. The rest of the year was spent at various circuses throughout the north of the country including a period in his home town of Warrington with his old friend Ohmy's Grand Circus in October, which then moved to Preston for the Christmas season. Harry Dale, 'the famous jester, whose quips and cranks are highly appreciated' appeared in a local report in Preston. The end of the year was spent in North Shields, on the north bank of the Tyne, where he had been appointed manager of Henry Alvo's Circus.

The *Shields Daily News* of 26 December 1900 stated:

> The new circus opened by Mr Henry Alvo in the Ropery Banks commenced its career auspiciously. The building was crowded and the programme was of a most attractive character. Graceful performance on the wires by the Sisters Lockhart, songs and imitations by Mr J.H. Kavanagh, comic cycling act by the Jacksons, a juggling act by the Sisters Oceanio, clever riding act by Miss Transfield, the Queen's Jester, Mr Harry Dale, and the Pyramid balancing king, Muns.

The season went on until the end of February 1901 giving three hours of entertainment for fourpence, sixpence, one shilling or two shillings. As manager, Harry Dale was responsible for selecting many of the acts so it was no coincidence that *The Stage* of 7 February reported an act named the Sisters Parez. Nepotism had arrived once again as the Parez Sisters were Ella, Lottie and Vera

Maud Dale, three of his daughters, who had also chosen the path of entertainment to make a living. At the conclusion of the season, a report in the *Shields Daily News* described a presentation to Harry Dale on his benefit night of a gold mounted inscribed umbrella 'which had been subscribed for by Mr Dale's admirers'. Sadly, I am not aware of the fate of this artefact, but an umbrella for use anywhere in Britain seems a very practical idea.

The year 1901 was significant in several ways starting with the death on 22 January of Queen Victoria at the age of eighty-one. After 63 years on the throne, she was the longest reigning monarch in British history. The newspapers were published with black borders and there was a feeling amongst the population that a great epoch had passed that could never be repeated. This was a period of transition in Britain with urbanisation and major changes in the countryside, a waning of religion, and the recognition that a new breed of men was now managing the population based not on hereditary right, but on money garnered from industry, mining, retailing, and so on.

The Empire mourned while the Boer War continued in South Africa moving towards its final phase of guerrilla warfare and a conclusion in May 1902, with the final surrender of the Boers.

The Queen's eldest son, the Prince of Wales, at the age of 60 became sovereign as Edward VII. He was a man of the world, in contrast to his reclusive mother. He was already well known to the audiences of the Victorian music halls and the circus as well as the racing fraternity. He was a man who liked to enjoy himself and amongst other attributes had been cited twice in court cases, which curiously added to his popularity. He seemed to release the people of Britain from a rather restrained existence which had been modelled on the old Queen herself. The Edwardian period was in marked contrast to what had gone before, and one group of beneficiaries was the entertainment profession. Edward VII delighted in the music hall and the theatre, and he saw no reason to change his habits after his coronation.

Moving on from North Shields, Harry Dale had a month in Great Grimsby with Dent's Grand Circus and lo and behold the Parez Sisters appeared again and 'gave a musical entertainment that is highly appreciated' according to *The Era* of 16 March.

The national census was taken on 31 March and the details for the Dale family were as follows:

Mill Lane, Warrington, Lancashire
Henry Thomas Dale, Head, Marr, Age 57, Vocalist
musician, b. Warwickshire, Birmingham
Sarah Ann Dale, Wife, Married, Age 49, Draper
shopkeeper, own account at home, b. Lancs, Liverpool
Ella Dale, Daughter, Single, Age 22 Professional
musician, b. Durham, Sunderland
Stanley Dale, Son, Single, Age 20, Gas stove finisher,
working, b. Lancs, Manchester
Lottie Dale, Daughter, Single, Age 17, Professional
musician, b. Yorks, Sheffield
Vera Maud Dale, Daughter, Single, Age 12, Professional
musician, b. Lancs. Manchester
Sydney Dale, Son, Single, Age 10, b. Lancs, Warrington
Doris Dale, Daughter, Single, Age 7, b. Lancs
Warrington.

It can be seen that four of the 10 living children are not listed. The two eldest boys, Albert and Harry Dale, were both now married, one living in Warrington, the other in Edinburgh, but at the time of the census they were abroad together performing as the 'Wamba Brothers' in South Africa. Amy Dale had married in 1895 and was living in Warrington with her husband Richard Bailey and their first child, Arnold. Finally, Ernest Dale had turned his back on show business and the family by joining the Royal Navy several years before, appearing in this census as an Able Seaman based in Chatham. Ella, Lottie and Vera Maud were listed as professional musicians and were making their name as the Parez Sisters on the music-hall stage and circus arena. Stanley Dale was making an honest living as a tanner and gas stove finisher but family lore informed me he was also known to be a skilled cornet/trumpet player, preferring the amateur status of the Warrington Borough Prize Band, rather than the professional stage. The main surprise in the census listing is Sarah Ann Dale described as 'draper shopkeeper, own account at home'. Her children were now of the age where they could fend for themselves, so probably to boost the family income, she had become an entrepreneur. I suspect with several family members needing stage costumes and other dressing requirements, she had turned her hand to dress making and no doubt had a good knowledge of drapery. Whether she had success in her venture is not known but later in this story she tried other means of raising money.

Harry Dale spent July and August by the sea in Blackpool at the Alhambra Circus; sharing the bill with Fraulein Grosvenor and her elephants, Monsieur Permane and his bears; the Florenze Troupe of acrobats; August & September, comedians; and the Yokohamas, jugglers, amongst others. Whilst in Blackpool he was interviewed for the *Blackpool Times* of 16 July by 'Leo' and the extensive article provided me with quite a lot of useful information about his early life which I have utilised in this history.

He was also interviewed at the end of July in Birmingham Assizes where Henry Lucas, a professional clown, sought to recover damages for libel from Harry Dale, described as a circus jester. The case was well reported – with some amusement – in *The Stage*, *The Era* and local papers such as *The Scotsman* in Edinburgh. Apparently, Lucas and Dale had been friends for many years and Lucas wrote to Dale in the spring of 1901 asking for employment in an entertainment company being formed by Harry Dale. Harry's reply was sent on a postcard from Great Grimsby accusing Lucas of copying some of his gags, jokes and repartee at other locations. He concluded by saying 'I will do my utmost to keep you out of estab-lishments where I go so that you will not work any more of my own gags.' In spite of a protest of innocence from Henry Lucas and a demand for an apology via Lucas' solicitors, Harry Dale chose to ignore the request. As a result, a court case was raised where the plaintiff's lawyer stated there was no copyright on patter and clowns often repeated gags and jokes heard from other performers. Harry Dale's lawyer argued the words used in the postcard were not libellous but the jury thought otherwise. Harry Dale lost the case and had to pay £30 damages. It may not seem much in modern money but using an average wage calculator table that sum works out as equivalent to about £12,500 in 2008. He had sent a rather expensive postcard to Lucas and illustrated once again an unfor-tunate streak of arrogance for which he paid, literally.

Undaunted, he set off again in September with appearances at the Hippodrome in Brighton and his three daughters performing with him once again for a week. At this time, Ella Dale was 23, Lottie was 18 and Vera Maud was only 13, but they were gaining popularity as a 'high class refined musical act'. After leaving Brighton in October he headed north east again to manage the

Borough Circus in North Shields for the festive season.

The proprietor of the Borough Circus was Arthur Jefferson, a name that achieved recognition and fame amongst music-hall aficionados then and still resonates today. In due course Jefferson left North Shields and relocated to Glasgow as the manager of the Scotia Music Hall in Stockwell Street. The great rival of this hall was the Britannia Music Hall in the Trongate, at that time owned and managed by A.E. Pickard. In 1906 a young man of 16 stepped onto the stage of the Britannia for the first time and gave an act as a comedian. Named Stanley Jefferson, he showed some promise so Pickard informed Jefferson about his son. Arthur Jefferson, in contrast, was shocked as he had no knowledge of his son's performance or abilities. Stanley Jefferson changed his name to Stan Laurel, emigrated to the United States and teamed up with Oliver Hardy. I like to think that when Harry Dale was the manager at the Borough Circus in 1901, he met 11 year old Stan Jefferson as he was then, and who knows, perhaps young Stan learnt a thing or two by watching the old pro at work in front of a live audience.

The Parez Sisters appeared at the Borough Circus for two weeks in December but headed off on their own to Glasgow and Bostock's Zoo Circus in January. Their father had placed an advert about the Parez Sisters in the 'Music Hall Cards' column of *The Era* on 26 October 1901. He was acting as their manager and he would be selecting the right opportunities for them until they gained confidence enough to manage themselves in due course.

The Borough Circus concluded in February 1902 so a return to Warrington with another circus ensued, then it was up to Carlisle with Algie's Circus once again. I need hardly add that his daughters appeared in Carlisle with him for a week and again later in the year at Ohmy's Circus in Preston. October had him in Wigan with the King's Circus while November saw him back on the music-hall stage for a week at the Empire Theatre of Varieties in Accrington. Was he keeping his music-hall hand in? Or more likely, did he have a free week between circus dates and this opportunity arose? We will never know, but virtually all his professional engagements were now with the various circuses and a music-hall appearance was a rare occurrence.

The end of 1902 had him back with Cooke's Circus in Edinburgh then he went on to Ohmy's Circus at Wigan again in the New Year. This pattern continued throughout 1903 with another diversion onto the music-hall stage in early December when he performed at the Empire, Hull, alongside his daughter Lottie Wamba who 'wins notice as a vocalist' with the Parez Trio, a further act on the same programme. Prior to that, he had placed an advert in *The Stage* dated 12 November seeking 'alfresco artists for the Isle of Man in June 1904'; contact point was his home address in Warrington: 32 Mill Lane.

From December 1903 until February 1904 he was manager of Harry Sloan's Circus in West Hartlepool bringing in acts such as Madame Louis, clairvoyant; Tao & Tai, jugglers; Allen McAskill, conjuror; Peter Simple, a clown; and Princess Annie, an expert hurdle rider. He also wrote and directed a novel sketch entitled 'Harum-Scarum or Raising Ructions' which 'created much amusement' according to *The Era* of 2 January 1904 whilst the *Northern Daily Mail* in January commented that Harry Dale 'was in good form with his smart sayings and witticisms and his imitations on the concertina were particularly successful'.

More management experience was gained in Carlisle in April and May at Algie's Hippodrome but there are no reports in any of the leading entertainment papers as to his summer activities. The advert back in November 1903 for 'alfresco artists for the Isle of Man' was probably the reason. I can only conjecture he was managing a number of acts somewhere on the island which was gaining recognition from the hard working populations of Lancashire, Cheshire and Yorkshire as a holiday destination.

Here he celebrated his 60th birthday in July and perhaps thoughts of retirement may have crossed his mind.

His name re-appeared in an advert in October 1904 claiming the position of hippodrome manager at Ohmy's Circus in Bolton, then in December through to March 1905 he was in Wales at Tonypandy Hippodrome titled 'General Manager & Ringmaster'. *The Stage* in January described the programme as 'a strong show' with acts such as the Eugenes, gymnasts; Mdme Florizel, the flexible Venus; the Salvanas, jugglers; Wha Pa Tee, Indian equestrian; Frank Hope, trick cyclist; and, of course, the Parez Sisters. Recycling his sketch 'Harum-Scarum' was 'highly diverting' according to *The Stage* of 9 February and he got a good benefit at the beginning of March when the show closed.

Family tragedy struck in July 1905, when Amy Bailey, his eldest child and daughter, died in Stockton Heath, near Runcorn, from a heart complication. She was only 33 and left a husband and four young children.

The rest of that year passed in the accustomed manner with management opportunities certainly taking priority over front line appearances. He seems to have had good relations with circus proprietors such as King Ohmy, Harry Sloan, Algie, and so on, and they asked him to manage their shows on a regular basis in a variety of capacities – general manager, ringmaster or equestrian director. I have no evidence he was tempted to establish his own circus as a sole, or even part proprietor, in spite of the fact that such a route was the way to make real money. He continued as a paid employee until he retired and possibly his poor upbringing in the Midlands reminded him of the times when money was in short supply. He had several faults, as I have illustrated in this story so far, but gambling does not seem to have been one of them. He did not gamble his future, or that of his family, in setting up his own business but perhaps there were reflective moments when he regretted not taking the plunge. By the age of 60, he was too late in any case; if he had made such a move it should have been in his late forties or early fifties.

The end of 1905 saw him back with Ohmy's Circus in Leigh, Lancashire, through to the beginning of 1906 when he returned to the stage for a week at the Wigan Hippodrome then moved to Emerson's Circus at Hull in April. There is little information about him during the rest of 1906 until an advert appeared in *The Era* dated 5 January 1907 under 'Circus Artists Wants':

> WANTED: Known to King Ohmy Circus, Hyde. We the undersigned thank you for paying full salaries although no performances on Christmas Day or night. John Irvine & Miss Pinder, Austin & Austin, Albert Troupe, Zola Troupe, A. Franic, Mlle Yvette, August & September, Harry Dale, Ringmaster.

Presumably King Ohmy was under no obligation to pay his circus entertainers on Christmas Day but chose to do so as a mark of respect and generosity to them. No doubt Ohmy getting a public 'thank-you' was good public relations by the performers for their future.

Ohmy had opened a brand new facility at Barrow on Furness

in late 1906 then moved the show to Hyde, near Manchester, and I think Harry Dale was his ringmaster at both locations. The season finished in late February 1907 but again I have little information about Harry's managerial appointments for the rest of this year.

One other diversity emerged in *The Stage* during July 1907 when his wife, Sarah Ann, advertised under the 'Apartments Vacant' column claiming:

> Warrington – Mrs Dale
> Comfortable homely rooms; bath and lavatory (h&c)
> 167 Knutsford Road

Was this a hobby situation, or was she short of money anticipating her husband's likely retirement? A rhetorical question but this advert, or something on similar lines, did appear several times in both *The Stage* and *The Era* from then on.

An announcement in *The Era* in December 1907 revealed that George Starr, the impresario and proprietor of the Crystal Palace in London, had engaged Gilleno's Continental Circus for the Festive Season. Amongst the acts were Whimsical Walker, the popular clown; the Four Ernests, equestrians; Harry Frisky, clown; the Mohamed Ben Mohamed Troupe of moors, feats of strength and agility; the Moras, triple bar performers; and Harry Dale the Court Jester who, according to *The Era* of 28 December, 'acts efficiently as Ringmaster and also provides an acceptable interlude as jester'.

An unusual gathering then took place at the Crystal Palace about 8 January 1908 when *The Stage* reported that there had been a luncheon with Whimsical Walker as chairman, involving 16 clowns dressed in their full attire. *The World's Fair* thought the menu of interest and it is reproduced here:

> Consomme Polchinelle
> Supreme de Barbue Acrobate
> Cote de Mouton Grimaldi
> Christmas Pudding Pierrot

As well as Whimsical Walker the clowns were Little Frisky, Funny Frisky, Little Danny, Frank Stevo, Happy Harry, Silly Silvo, Tom Verty, D'Almar, Jolly Lewis, Spud Murphy, Funny Fred, Tom Olmar, Silly Willy, Leo Vascrott and, of course, Harry Dale. At the conclusion of the lunch the usual loyal toasts were proposed by Whimsical Walker and Little Frisky while Harry Dale proposed a toast to the 'Press and Guests'. Mr Starr then responded and the proceedings terminated with the singing of the old clown song and chorus led by Harry Dale: 'Keep your Thumbs and Fingers Moving.' It seems a good time was had by all!

Gilleno's Circus was a great success and its original engagement was prolonged into early February. On 1 February in *The Era*, the Four Ernests publicly thanked Mr Gilleno, Mr F. Connor (equestrian director), Harry Dale and Whimsical Walker for 'helping to make it a most happy season'. In March, Gillenos moved to the garrison town of Aldershot, finishing the season there.

I have been unable to find any references to Harry Dale during the summer months of 1908 but assume he was acting as a manager or ringmaster at two or three circuses in the country somewhere. By November, John Henry Cooke was seeking acts for his Edinburgh circus season and his musical director, Harry Wamba (Harry Dale junior) was seeking musicians for the orchestra. Cooke's Circus opened for the season on 21 November and I was delighted to find that Mr Harry Dale, now aged 64, was engaged for the season working with his son who was now thirty-three. My father, Bert Dale, was born in April 1908 in Edinburgh, so I hope his grandfather entertained him at home in the same style that he entertained the Edinburgh audiences from November 1908 through to February 1909!

The Stage and *The Era* reported on John Henry Cooke's Circus including his 'spectacular pantomime' entitled 'King Gold and the Lucky Little Lassie' where the part of 'King Gold – a genial King – was played by Harry Dale, and Princess Sovereign by Miss Cora Irene'. In late January the pantomime finished and was replaced by 'Dick Turpin's Ride to York' which ran through to the end of February where the final entry in *The Era* of 20 February paid tribute to Mr Harry Dale, 'equally at home as jester, vocalist and instrumentalist'. This was really his swan song, as he now retired from the entertainment business in his 65th year after some 40 years in the profession.

But the family which he headed was still busy. Harry Wamba continued as Cooke's musical director for another couple of years; the Parez Sisters, now a well regarded skilful and versatile act were all about to get married; and Albert Wamba (Dale) and his wife

Martha Dorothy, performing as either 'Les Wambas' or 'La Belle Lily & Albert' were also a successful music-hall/circus act.

A year of Dale marriages took place in 1909. During his sojourn in Edinburgh, another of Harry's sons had married. Stanley Henry Dale, aged 28 and a journeyman tanner, married Mary Harper, aged 22, in the Parish Church of St James in Latchford, Warrington. On 20 April 1909 in Warrington, Ella Dale, the eldest of the Parez Trio, married an actor Gus Patrick Coyne, while shortly thereafter on 8 May in the Register Office of Lanchester, Co. Durham, a double wedding took place with Lottie Dale aged 25 marrying John Hindmarsh Howarth, an electrician, and Vera Maud Dale aged 20, marrying Walter Lawson, another electrician, who in due course became a successful operator of several cinemas in north east England.

The 1911 census revealed Harry and his wife were in residence at 16 Ash Grove in Warrington, and as all parents know full well, no matter what age they are, you never see the last of your children. Sharing the house with them on census night were Albert and his wife Martha, Ernest, and finally Doris May. Albert and Martha's daughter, Mercia Dale, was living with Martha's mother in Cheshire. The 1911 census was the first to show the actual hand writing of the head of household who completed the official form. Harry Dale's hand writing is not strong, so perhaps age – he was 67 – was starting to catch up with him.

About a year later, a further marriage took place on 15 January, 1912 in Warrington, when his third oldest son, Ernest, discharged from the Royal Navy in 1909 after 12 years service, married a widow, Carrie Counsel. Later that year there was a further tragedy in the family when Albert Dale's beloved wife, the gymnast Martha Dorothy, died suddenly from a tropical disease, possibly malaria, in Sumatra in September whilst they were on tour with a circus.

Harry Dale could spend his retirement in his home in Warrington with a feeling of modest satisfaction that he had been a performer of some note, and had provided for his family materially, as well as educating them competently.

To complete his life story, he and his wife moved to Slater Street, quite close to Ash Grove, in Latchford, Warrington, until he travelled to visit his daughter Vera Maud Lawson and her husband in Ashington, Northumberland in March 1914. In his 70th year he died suddenly in Ashington at 22 Council Road from a heart condition, pleurisy and broncho-pneumonia on 20 March. He is buried in the Holy Sepulchre Church cemetery in Ashington but sadly the stone above his grave has now disappeared. There was no will but a Letter of Administration dated 6 April 1914 left a modest sum of £60 to his widow. In modern money that is about £21,600 – not a great deal to show for 40 years entertaining audiences throughout the British Isles and other parts of the world.

An obituary was written in *The World's Fair* of 25 April 1914. It was perhaps not as accurate as it should have been, nevertheless it was a moving tribute:

DEATH OF HARRY DALE
Well Known Circus Manager

Harry Dale, the jester, who has just passed away at the age of 69, after an illness of one week's duration, from pneumonia and pleurisy, was a native of Birmingham. Prior to entering the arenic profession, he worked the halls as a musical jester, playing the musical glasses and concertina and singing his own compositions 'Does thy Heart beat True to me?', 'Silver Bells', etc. His first appearance in the ring was in Aberdeen with Mr John Henry Cooke in 1882 as a musical clown. He was well known in Lancashire in connection with Ohmy's Circus, following 'Fritz', the jester as manager. He retired from the business about five years ago, his last engagement being with Mr Cooke in Edinburgh, taking a public house in Warrington, which we do not think was a success.

His son, Harry Wamba, is a clever conductor, having fourteen years with John Henry Cooke's Circus, also with Mr E. Bostock and other shows. The other members of the family the Sisters Perry (*sic*), Wamba Brothers, and Albert of Lily & Albert, hold good positions in the music hall world.

Like most of us, he had his failings, cynical and hasty, but straight as a die, with a heart that responded to the cause of charity if deserving. May he rest in peace.

Most people would agree that life is never ordered, and Harry Dale's was no exception. He had a cocktail of happiness, sadness, success and failure, strokes of luck and periods of concern, but his life was certainly not boring.

An interesting article was published on 22 October 1927 in *The World's Fair* bemoaning the demise of the traditional circus and its performers. The writer, code-named GES, asks the question: 'Who would listen to a jester to-day?' Then answers his own question: 'The jester is right out of fashion. The last two jesters in England were David Abbey Seal and Harry Dale. The cap and bells are on the shelf and will stop there for a long time.' A sentiment I cannot argue against. As David Abbey Seal died in 1898, Harry Dale was the last Edwardian Jester!

And what of his first wife, Emma Dale née Davis? She seems to have led a quiet life with her surviving son John Dale in Wolverhampton throughout the lifetime of Harry Dale. She was a 'shop girl' on her marriage certificate in 1864 then became a 'tray polisher' in a 'tin wire works' in each census until 1911, the last one currently available. I have no idea if she had any contact with Harry Dale. I think she had a sad life as she lost three children in the early days of her marriage. Her son Charles Dale, fathered by Harry Dale, died in 1891; and her other son, John Dale, father unknown, survived. Emma died in Wolverhampton on 13 November 1919 aged 73, although her son, John, stated she was 72 on the death certificate. She died at 27 Old Mill Street, an area of Wolverhampton she had lived in most of her adult life. The entry in the certificate under the column 'Occupation' reads: 'Widow of Harry Dale, a general labourer'. Did her son John, know the true story? Or had she hidden the truth from him all these years – he was 43 when she died, and he passed away in Wolverhampton, unmarried, in June 1938 aged 62. I will never know.

My grandfather, Harry Wamba Dale, had four sons. The eldest, another Harry Dale was born in 1901, the next in line was John Lavin Dale born in 1903, the third was born in 1905 and died in 1907; his name was Charles William Dale, and the fourth son was my father Albert Stanley Ernest Dale born in 1908. The forename 'John' is found in the Dale family tree in the early days, so no real surprise there, but there is no 'Charles' in the family tree anywhere except for the 'Charles' who died in 1891. Perhaps my grandfather knew the story as he would be a contemporary of Emma Dale and her son John, and for his own reasons, named two of his children after his half brothers, in the same way as he gave my father the forenames of three of his full brothers. This is a conspiracy theory on my part, but every family has secrets, and mine is no exception!

Harry Dale's second wife, Sarah Ann Dale, lived on until 1931 dying on 9 May aged 80 at the home of her youngest daughter, Doris May Lemon, at 9 Monks Street, Warrington. She is interred in Warrington Cemetery but again the stone above her grave has disappeared. I think she was a pillar of strength, holding the Dale family together in good times and bad. There are a few photographs of her with various family members – her small size is noticeable but her loyalty to her husband and her children was enormous. I must assume she knew of the bigamy of Henry Thomas Dale, perhaps from the first day she met him, but she went through a ceremony of marriage and stood by him for over 40 years. She is a lady I admire a great deal.

So the lasting memorials to Harry and Sarah Ann are not found carved in stone above their final resting places but are in their extensive family and the many descendants spread throughout the world.

THE BROTHERS WAMBA

I have noted in a previous chapter that Mr Harry Dale is reputed to have written at least 300 music-hall songs during his career, the majority of which are long forgotten. Another, perhaps more lasting, achievement with which he can be identified was the procreation of children. In his first, and legitimate marriage to Emma Davis, he definitely fathered three children: Rosanna, Sarah Ann and Charles Dale, with a possible addition of John Dale, but I have my doubts about Harry Dale being the father of this last one. Both the girls died comparatively young leaving Charles and John to make their own way in the world. However, Harry's second 'marriage' to Sarah Ann Edgington produced a much more impressive total of 11 children, 10 of whom survived – five boys and five girls. The first child appeared in 1872 and the last in 1893. With the high infant death rate in Victorian times, this in itself was quite impressive, although his wife, Sarah Ann, was probably more prais-worthy in this respect than him.

With both Harry Dale and his wife engaged in the enter-tainment business, it is no surprise that several of their children, chose the same route to make a living. Many Victorian and Edwardian performers did exactly the same thing, as they had contacts, could open doors, and were able to train and nurture their offspring to suit audience demand in a highly competitive business.

Three of Harry's boys and four of the girls chose to become professionals in show business and each, in their own way, achieved some success. None of them could be called top of the range enter-tainers, but I think they played to their strengths. I am going to concentrate on the boys in the next chapter or two as my own grandfather, Harry Wamba Dale, was amongst them and he provided a solid platform for my father and his siblings in later life.

The five boys born in chronological order were Albert (1873), Harry (1875), Ernest (1877), Stanley Henry (1880) and Sydney Edgar (1890). Albert, Harry and Sydney chose to be entertainers, whilst Ernest Dale joined the navy, and Stanley Henry Dale, although a skilled musician, worked in industry.

Albert Dale was born on 28 February 1873 at 20 Shaw Street, Oldham in Lancashire. His father, Harry Dale, described himself as a 'file-cutter' on the birth certificate although by 1873 he was well established on the music hall circuit. The census returns for 1881 showed the Dale family now living in Manchester at 112 Ridgeway Street, and Albert aged eight, is described as a scholar. I had little further information about his early life until, by chance, I came across a book in a charity shop in Edinburgh written by Anna Blair, a Glasgow author, in which oral recollections of older people in Glasgow had been brought together. There was a chapter about entertainment and amongst those interviewed was a man named Alan Stuart Dale, a retired cinema manager, who described the early life of his father in some detail and I recognised immediately that his father was Albert Dale. Not only did this fill a gap in my knowledge of my Dale family, but after a bit of detective work, I was delighted to make contact with a clan of Dales in the West of Scotland whose current generation emerged as my second cousins. Apparently, Albert ran away to sea aged 12 and worked in America for a spell. He seems to have had some natural musical talent and came back to England. He is recorded in the 1891 census as living with the Dale family in the Victoria Hotel, Stockport, Cheshire, at that time managed by his father. Albert, aged 18, and his younger brother Harry, aged 16, are both described as 'bar tenders'. There is no doubt they both received intensive musical tuition from their father. However, the important feature of Albert's life was pairing up with his brother Harry, and forming a duo of musical clowns known as 'The Brothers Wamba'. A stage name was essential for the two sons of Harry Dale as he was well enough known in the business, so another 'Harry Dale' would have caused some confusion.

Those readers who are fans of Sir Walter Scott's historical novels may recall that in the first chapter of *Ivanhoe*, a character is introduced who had 'thin silver bracelets on his arms, and on his neck a collar of the same metal, bearing the inscription: 'Wamba, son of Witless, is the thrall of Cedric of Rotherwood'. Later, in chapter seven, he describes himself as 'Wamba, son of Witless, son of Weatherbrain, who was the son of an Alderman'. Wamba, although acting the fool and a jester to Cedric the Saxon, turned out to be a brave fool and rubbed shoulders with the forester Locksley – better known as Robin Hood – and his companion Allan-a-Dale. Hopefully, the reader will recognise the clever ploy of naming his two sons the Brothers Wamba, but I certainly have never regarded Harry Dale, the father, as 'Witless'.

At this point I need to summarise briefly Harry Wamba Dale's early life. Albert and Harry followed a pattern in their formative years that was surprisingly close. Harry Dale, the second boy, and my grandfather, was born at 19 Eden Street, Oldham on 26 January 1875. The story goes that he was also a talented musician from an early age and had a major argument with a music teacher at his school. Father Dale agreed with his son in this argument, and he never went back to school, so his father found him a musical post in the Bellevue Orchestra in Manchester.

The Wamba Brothers partnership concentrated on musical comedy and both brothers became skilled performers on a number of different instruments. Albert Dale's speciality was the saxophone and clarinet, whilst Harry Dale, concentrated on the cornet/ trumpet. As their act developed they played additional instruments and also manufactured fantastic instruments of bent tubes and ridiculous shapes from which they coaxed delightful music. The hand of their father is obvious in this act as he was a talented musician himself and perhaps he identified a gap in the market where his two sons could develop and exploit their skills.

The earliest reference I have found is in *The Era* dated 13 March 1897 where an advert by the Brothers Wamba claims: 'only good instruments well played, good songs sung, twenty five minute act and God Save the Queen and Circus Proprietors'. A comment here on Queen Victoria's Diamond Jubilee enhancing the patriotic fervour that was sweeping the country at the time. A week later a similar advert claims: 'the following instruments are well played: guitar, mandoline, double handbells, double fairy bells, double organ pipes, double banjos, cornet, English concertina, violin, post horn, monster tubulars'. An astonishing number of instruments and important that they played them well in front of highly critical Victorian audiences, otherwise their reputation would suffer. Fortunately, a family photograph has survived showing the huge range of instruments they played and it has occurred to me that carrying all this paraphernalia with them when they had an engagement must have been physically exhausting as well as a

The Wamba Brothers. Albert on left, Harry on right, central figure unknown, *c.*1901 (Dale Collection)

financial burden in transport terms.

A further advert the next week reflects their sense of self depre-cating humour by concluding:

Good music, good instruments, good songs, good voices, good appearance, good salaries, good boys. 1 Amelia Street, Warrington.

Their advertising campaign paid off as they appeared with John Henry Cooke's Circus in Arbroath in early September moving to

Range of instruments used by the Wamba Brothers (Dale Collection)

Perth in late September where their father also appeared as 'The Prince of Jesters'. The developing musical talent of Harry Wamba Dale, aged 22, emerged in Perth where as well as appearing in his own right as one of the Brothers Wamba, he was billed as the musical director of the circus orchestra under the name 'Harry Wamba'. Their popularity in Cooke's Circus was revealed in a further *Era* advert dated 2 April 1898 when they were performing with the circus in Kilmarnock, 'just completing engagement of 46 weeks with John Henry Cooke. 86 weeks in two years with one concern'. I have no doubts that nepotism assisted their careers and gave them a foothold on the ladder, but there was nothing unusual about this and Cooke would not have retained them if their act had been poor or unpopular.

Back with Cooke in Edinburgh at the end of 1898 a *Scotsman* report of 15 November comments: 'Without this house of entertainment, the places of amusement in Edinburgh would be incomplete ... a full and interesting programme ... towards the enjoyment of the evening the orchestra under Mr Harry Wamba contributed largely.'

Albert however, had fallen in love and the two brothers had to accept some changes in their lives. Whilst performing in a circus, which I think might have been Cooke's in Perth in late 1897, Albert met a young lady gymnast named Martha Dorothy Blackmore. She was born in 1876 and was therefore three years younger than him. She was part of a family act which came from Liverpool and her father, William Blackmore, modestly described himself as a professor of gymnastics in the 1891 census. The family was called the Fernandez Troupe and they appeared in various circuses over a long period of time. Gymnastics was a generic term that included such skills as the trapeze and the two lovers did a very interesting thing! Albert, a musician, trained himself to become a trapeze artist like his girlfriend, and she, a gymnast, trained herself to become a musician like her boyfriend. The result was two quite different acts provided by the same duo – but I am running ahead of time.

Albert Dale married Martha Dorothy Blackmore on 19 January 1899 at Holy Trinity Church, Wavertree, Liverpool and they had a daughter born on 10th November the same year in Liverpool whom they named Dorothy Mercia Victoria Dale. The family origins in the ancient kingdom of Mercia, centred on Wolverhampton, emerged in her name, and in later life she was always known as 'Mercia'.

Harry Dale, not to be outdone by his brother, waited until the circus season finished on Monday 13 February 1899 and was married on 15 February to Jane Lavin by a Sheriff's Warrant (Special Licence) at 63 Cockburn Street, Edinburgh. Jane Lavin, was always known as 'Jeannie' and was the younger daughter of Patrick Lavin, a poor immigrant Irish labourer from County Leitrim and Maggie Ferguson, his wife, a country girl born in Keith, Banffshire in the north east of Scotland. How Harry and Jeannie met is not known as she was not in the entertainment business, being only a 'confectioner's assistant' on the marriage certificate, but it may be that the Lavins took in circus professionals during the season as their house in the Grassmarket was well located in proximity to Cooke's Circus establishment. I found it interesting that the two brothers married within a month of each other, and have often wondered if there was a strong competitive element between these two siblings! Harry and Jeannie Dale had a daughter born on 24 January 1900 at 36 Grassmarket, Edinburgh, the home of her parents. Sadly the baby died within a few hours and was never named.

Although the two brothers were now domiciled in different

parts of the country – Harry and Jeannie in Edinburgh, and Albert and Martha in Warrington, Lancashire – they must have linked closely as they performed as a duo in various locations within Britain.

From Scotland they had moved to Southport with Wirth's Circus in April 1898 then to Hyde with Transfield's Circus alongside their father once again. After a period with Paddock's Royal British Circus they appeared with Batty's Circus in Stockton on Tees over the festive season then had a spell on the music-hall stage in the Gaiety, West Hartlepool, in February 1899 where the local reporter stated: 'The Brothers Wamba were exceedingly clever and should not be missed.' The Oxford Theatre in Middlesbrough followed in March, then there was York in early April and a return to John Henry Cooke's Circus in Greenock later that month. The *Greenock Herald* of 27 May stated that 'the entertaining pair produced music from all manner of instruments from the piano down to the Chinese pipes and their efforts were received with prolonged applause.' They continued with Cooke appearing in Kirkcaldy in October, then Edinburgh for the opening of the festive season again in November.

In 1900 they had three weeks in South Shields at Algie's Circus in March then went back to Greenock with Cooke alongside the Brothers Leotard, Teddy Saul and his Arab Acrobats and Cooke's two sons, D'Alberto and Douglas, well regarded clowns and equestrians.

Harry Dale, the Wamba's father, had recently returned from South Africa so it was no surprise when the situation there turned in favour of the Imperial Army, that entertainment became more relevant for the long suffering population.

The Boer War between the British and the Burghers of the Transvaal and the Orange Free State commenced in October 1899. After several setbacks, the imperial troops started to make progress in early 1900 with the relief of Kimberley taking place in February and Mafeking in May of the same year, although it was May of 1902 before the Boers finally surrendered.

Transcript details of the SS *Goth* sailing from Southampton to Cape Town, South Africa on 7 July 1900 reveals 'Mr H. Wamba' and 'Mr A. Wamba' as passengers along with a number of other circus entertainers.

An advertisement in *The Era* for 1 August 1900 under the

heading 'Amusements in South Africa' draws attention to the Imperial Circus of Mr & Mrs A. Bonamici which opened later that month in Cape Town. 'An excellent temporary building at Dock Road and a really first rate company' on the opening night kept some 2,000 people in good humour from start to finish. Amongst the performers were the 'Brothers Wamba, eccentric musical clowns and talented artists'. I have no in depth background to this circus but it seems to have been a morale booster for the English-speaking Cape Colony, where the war must have restricted entertainment and created difficult times for the people. Arthur Bonamici was a well-regarded impresario having lived in South Africa for some 20 years, and a report in *The Stage* of 20 April 1899 praised his initiative in bringing over a range of entertainment in spite of the worsening relations between the Boers and the government in Britain.

With positive progress on the military side, the appearance of the circus was probably arranged between Bonamici and the relevant authorities. After a few weeks at Cape Town they finished at the end of September, and the circus moved north to Kimberley where Cecil Rhodes had been isolated because of the siege, but was now re-opening his mines. From there they moved east to East London in Natal and then to Durban in the early part of 1901. At this time, an interesting letter was published in *The Era* dated the 23rd March 1901 from Albert Wamba. To paraphrase, he defends Bonamici as there were rumours that the company was stranded, the artists were not receiving their salaries and at least one performer was working his passage home to Britain. Albert Wamba strenuously denied these rumours but did describe some of their movements about the country as difficult, including living in a captured Boer railway carriage for three weeks. He reminded the readers that at this time 'martial law is in force almost everywhere'. He wrote the letter from Durban where 'we are now enjoying ourselves and seeing the country'. He concludes by saying, 'We are happy and comfortable and I trust these few words will be a means of dispelling all misconceptions as to our position in South Africa.'

Albert's wife, Martha Dorothy, sailed from Southampton for Natal on 27 April 1901 to join her husband and brother-in-law. Her daughter, Mercia, is not listed amongst the passengers, so presumably she was left behind with relations.

The Brothers Wamba continued the tour well into 1901 and earned this from *The Natal Witness* of 3 July 1901 – 'The Brothers

Wamba in their fiddle entrée reduced the divine art of music to absurdity. Many musicians who are lauded for their pizzicato movements etc could learn something from the Brothers Wamba.' Praise indeed!

A couple of photographs exist (see p.77) showing Albert and Harry clowning around in a photographic studio. There is a third man in these photographs who is unknown but the two Dale brothers are smartly dressed and obviously having a bit of fun. These photographs are dated about this period and might even have been taken in South Africa.

On 28 September 1901 Albert, Martha and Harry disembarked at Southampton from the Union Castle Mail Steamship Company vessel, SS *Gascon*. As a memento, the brothers had each received a silver medal from Arthur Bonamici and at least one of these medals remains in the Dale family up to the present day. In addition, Harry Wamba Dale would meet his second child, a boy christened, inevitably, Harry Dale, born on 17 March 1901 at 36 Grassmarket in Edinburgh. No doubt his father-in-law, an Irishman named Patrick, would be delighted with the birth of his first grandson on St Patrick's Day. This child was the fourth generation to bear the name 'Harry' or 'Henry', and he was my father's eldest brother.

Having been out of the public eye for several months it was essential that Albert and Harry got their name back into circulation. An advert in *The Era* for 5 October 1901 indicates they 'will be at liberty from October 14th, halls, circuses, home or abroad'. The contact address was 19 Coleridge Street, Liverpool, the home of Albert's in-laws, the Blackmore family. The adverts continued for the next couple of weeks such as:

THE SPARKLING GEMS FROM KIMBERLEY

The Brothers Wamba, South African Musical Comedians. Ready for work Monday next October 14th after well earned holiday. Vacant for pantomimes. La Belle Lily and Clown Albert, Natal gymnasts, in conjunction with above. Wire: 19 Coleridge Street, Liverpool.

This advert is the first evidence I have that Albert and his wife Martha Dorothy were developing a new act where he, the talented musician, became the 'strong man' in a trapeze act. It will become clear later that she transformed herself into a useful musician and by combining their talents, they could offer a double act, but I am not sure if they were paid twice when performing on a programme with both acts!

Modesty was not a Dale attribute, so mimicking their father's approach, they blew their own trumpet with the following advert dated 19 October 1901:

BROTHERS WAMBA.
South African Musical Comedians. Funniest of Funny Musicians. Grotesque Pianists, Silly Fiddlers, Harmonious Footballers, Mirth Provoking Handbell Ringers etc.
Also La Belle Lily, Gymnastic Queen & Clown Albert.

The result was a response and they performed at North Shields Borough Circus at the end of October where it may be remembered the manager was their father and the proprietor was Arthur Jefferson. Engagements thereafter were slow to come in spite of a continual barrage of adverts which included choice copy such as 'Colonial Musical Comedians', 'Musical Wonders', 'Trans-Equatorial Musical Marvels' etc. The impression they were giving was that they were actually South African in origin rather than a couple of lads born in Oldham. Perhaps they were cashing in on the patriotic fervour that was sweeping the country as the imperial troops gradually overcame the Boers.

By January 1902 they were performing in the New South London Palace of Varieties and in February they were in Bostock's Circus in Warrington followed in March by an appearance with Bostock's Zoo Circus in Glasgow. The Palace in Derby in April came next then the Grand Circus in Great Grimsby where both the Brothers Wamba and La Belle Lily and Albert performed.

At about this time I think Albert and Harry realised their act was not achieving the success they had hoped. I do not have an exact date, but the Brothers Wamba disappeared to be replaced by The Wambas. In essence, this meant Harry Wamba Dale had gone and Albert and his wife now established themselves with two acts, one musical, the other gymnastic.

Harry Wamba Dale returned to Edinburgh and his wife and family, and concentrated on his musical abilities as a circus orchestra musical director. His career will be examined in a later chapter but for the next few years, La Belle Lily & Albert and The Wambas prospered on both the music hall stage and the circus arena.

It would be tedious to list the many performances they gave throughout the country where in some locations they appeared as 'The Wambas', with music the focus, and in other locations as 'La Belle Lily and Albert' with their trapeze act. On several occasions they appeared as both and in every case seemed to be well received. As mentioned elsewhere, they were popular with John Henry Cooke for several years, with many performances in his circus in locations throughout Scotland and elsewhere.

By 1904/05 they were advertising their act regularly in *The Era* so their weekly or fortnightly performances can be followed with ease. During 1905 for example, there was a week in Belfast at the Alhambra then two weeks in The Tivoli in Dublin followed by a week in Dewsbury's Hippodrome. Dundee's Gaiety Theatre followed, with a spell by the seaside at Morecambe's Central Pier then on to Sunderland for two weeks at the Olympia, a final dash to Dumfries and the Theatre Royal then back to Edinburgh for a season with Cooke again through November, December and January, concluding in early February 1906. Whilst in Edinburgh, they lived at 36 Grassmarket, the home of Harry and Jeannie Dale who by this time had three young sons sharing the space with the grandparents, Patrick and Maggie Lavin. It must have been a crowded household!

As can be seen by this example, their lives were full of motion as they moved round these many locations living in theatrical digs with only the Sunday free for rest, travel and relaxation. At least with a season in the circus they had a regular income but for an act like theirs, they had to keep fit and practice constantly. It was a hard life with little outside interest and the great fear was probably illness. Albert and Martha only had one living child, Mercia. The 1911 census revealed that Martha had had another child who had died. A further pregnancy would have terminated their trapeze act but they did have the option of the musical act and Albert in his own right was a clever clown, musician and comic, who could have performed solo if required. It was not to be, however, so they continued with their acts for the next two to three years.

Albert and Martha Dorothy returned to Warrington from Edinburgh where they were now domiciled at Knutsford Road. It is worth mentioning here that three substantial changes took place in the entertainment business between 1900 and 1914 that affected all in the profession.

Starting after the turn of the century and developing over the next few years, many of the larger music halls throughout Britain had been purchased by major entertainment chains. Significant operators in this sector included Moss Varieties, Oscar Stoll, McNaughton Vaudeville, Barrasford Ltd, the London Theatre of Varieties, and the De Frece Circuit. The result of this was that many acts, operating through agents, were booked for many weeks by these chains giving these performers security and income, giving the music-hall theatres bookings well in advance, but giving lesser known acts more problems in obtaining bookings. The Wambas fell into this latter category as they were their own agents, hence the constant advertising on a weekly basis in the trade press. It also meant if they were not booked by the big chains, they were excluded from the major music halls mainly in the larger cities and towns. It is noticeable that their bookings from about 1906 onwards moved towards the smaller, independent halls in smaller towns. Another factor which has been mentioned earlier, was the gradual expansion of the 'bioscope', or films, as they became known. Still in black and white and silent, these early short films were now shown quite commonly at the end of music-hall evenings and in the circus. Audiences were treated to the latest news in the Empire, events, celebrations, comic situations and a host of other subjects many of which were topical and relevant to their lives. This was the thin end of the wedge that eventually brought about the decline of the music hall.

Another lesser phenomenon was the 'concert party' where a well known entertainer would provide a music hall proprietor with a complete programme package of entertainment recruited and managed by him. Usually these concert parties were focused on the leading entertainer who was not against bringing members of his family and friends into the supporting acts. A couple of examples of this inclusive approach were shows by Arthur Lloyd and Dr Walford Bodie. Again, it was difficult for the independent acts to get into this circuit, so there was a progressive and gradual decline in the options open to such performers.

To illustrate this gradual change, the 1906 season saw the Wambas in the latter half of the year perform in the Princes

Theatre, Llandudno; Wakefield Hippodrome; the Empire in Wrexham; the Central Pier in Morecambe; in Glasgow at a series of 'harmonic concerts'; the Palace Theatre, Dundee; the Baths, Hoddesdon; the Palace Theatre in Boston then finally at the Hippodromes in Scarborough followed by Great Yarmouth. A strenuous south Wales tour in early 1907 saw them in The Temperance Hall in Merthyr Tydfil; the Palace Theatre in Porth; the Pavilion in Carmarthen; then they moved to Maesteg and finished in Treherbert. All done without the benefit of motor transport, relying on the train service and probably a horse and cart. The logistics of some of these tours beggars belief.

The 1911 census on 2 April revealed that Albert and Martha were staying with his father and mother at 16 Ash Grove, in Warrington. They were destined to sail to the Far East in June so perhaps had no immediate engagements. The upbringing of their daughter, Mercia, seems to have been left to Martha's mother, Mary Blackmore, now a widow of 68, as the census showed she and Mercia, aged 11, were staying together at Liscard in Cheshire. Mercia was described as being at school. It must have been difficult for her being detached from her parents but Albert and Martha's nomadic life was not suitable for a young child, and she had at least stability living with her grandmother.

It is no surprise therefore that when an opportunity came along to travel abroad with a circus, they seized it. They followed in the footsteps of Albert's father, Harry Dale, by travelling to the Far East with a circus, but unfortunately I am unable to name it. I think they left the shores of Britain in late 1911 and visited the British possessions in Singapore and the Straits Settlements moving on to the islands of Java and Sumatra. Sadly, tragedy struck whilst on this tour. Albert's wife, Martha Dorothy died suddenly from some form of tropical disease, possibly malaria. Details of the British Consular Returns of Births, Marriages and Deaths are available online and her death was recorded in Sumatra on 19 September 1912. The death certificate shows her death on board the SS *Elont* bound for Belawan on the East coast of Sumatra. She was 37 years old and the informant was her husband, Albert, 'presently residing at the Medan Hotel, Medan.' The vice consul at Medan, Mr A.H. Mathewson, recorded all the details. The official death certificate does not state the cause of death but an obituary notice was published in *The Era* on 26 October 1912:

Deaths:
DALE. Martha Dorothy, the well beloved wife of Albert
Dale (Les Wambas) passed peacefully away at sea in the
Malacca Straits of malaria fever. She lies at rest in the
cemetery of Medan, Sumatra.
God's will be done.

Albert was devastated, especially as he had to bury her there in
Sumatra. He erected a commemorative stone over her grave, and
photographs were taken, but these were lost, when a fire destroyed
much of the family memorabilia in the 1960s. Albert himself
travelled back on the SS *Goeben* from Penang to Southampton as a
third-class passenger arriving on 7 November 1912.

I have no certain knowledge of what he did in the months
immediately after his return but I believe the bottle was his
companion for a period. He had his daughter, Mercia, now aged 13,
and she must have been some consolation for him. I did find some
evidence in April 1913 in *The Era* that he sought a means of earning
a living. An advert appeared on 12 April stating

THE WAMBA BROTHERS
A new idea in musical acts.
Own scenery and effects.
264 Knutsford Road, Warrington.

I was surprised at this, as it meant his brother Harry had put aside
his musical directorship in Lord John Sanger's circus (see next
chapter) and was again working with his brother. The advert
appeared again on 19 April and a report was found the week after
for the Clydebank Theatre, owned by the Glasgow entrepreneur,
A.E. Pickard, where it stated:

This week, twice nightly. La Belle Tosca, wire performer;
Gallagher & West, comedians; W.H. Smart, comedian; the
Wamba Brothers in a musical novelty, and pictures.

On 3 May a report in *The Era* is given for the Casino Theatre in
Glasgow, another establishment owned by A.E. Pickard, where the
Wamba Brothers topped the bill supported by the Greenlees,
operatic duettists; and Bertha Travis, comedienne.

Further searching did not reveal any more performances of the duo, but the plot thickened when I found a 23 July 1913 advert for 'The Three Dales, in their refined artistic music and vocal act' where they performed in the Empire, Wrexham and then in Ashton. Was this Albert, Harry and perhaps Albert's daughter, Mercia?

Some 18 months after Albert's return to Britain, the First World War started in August 1914. I have found references to 'Les Wambas' performing in November 1914 at the Hippodrome, Peterborough

Mercia Wamba (Dale), Albert's daughter. Aged 14 or 15 about 1915 (Dale Collection)

and his partner in the act was his young daughter, Mercia. An advert in *The Stage* for 19 November 1914 states:

LES WAMBAS
La Petite Belle Mercia et Albert

Pot-pourri. Double gymnastic and musical act.
A novel and versatile performance.
This week Hippodrome, Wisbech.
Permanent 15 Beechwood Avenue, Warrington.

It would seem therefore, that Albert and his daughter were duplicating the act created with his late wife. A photo exists (see opposite) of Mercia Dale, showing an attractive young lady dressed as a trapeze artist. She looks confident, is slender, and I believe she was quite small, perhaps just over five feet tall. In 1914 she was 14 while her father was 41.

Unlike the Second World War, there was no move by the government to close the music halls when the war started. After all, there was an expectation it would all be over by Christmas. How wrong they were!

An advert in *The Stage* dated 25 February 1915 posed the question:

Why engage foreigners when you have Britishers not as good, but better?

ALBERT WAMBA AND DAUGHTER MERCIA
Sensational Gymnasts & Comedy Instrumentalists.

A unique combination of Calisthenics and Music
Forming a novel and versatile performance.
The Empire Torquay, next Empire Tredegar
Perm. Add. 15 Beechwood Avenue, Warrington.

They continued their perambulations around the country with September 1915 spent at the Picture House in Lurgan, then in Belfast at the Coliseum, while January 1916 saw them in the Royal Agricultural Hall, Islington where they had added 'Sensational Demon Bagpipers' to their repertoire.

However, the call of King and Country reached Albert and he enrolled as a volunteer on 18 April 1916 at the East Claremont Drill Hall in Edinburgh joining the 3/9 Battalion, Royal Scots. His younger brother Harry was already a serving soldier in this battalion, and both brothers were utilised in the battalion military band.

Full details of his Attestation and Medical Record have survived showing he was 43 years 1 month old on volunteering, was 5'4" tall and had a chest measurement of 36.5 inches. He had brown hair, grey eyes, and was described as a 'gymnast' and his next of kin was his daughter, Mercia. Following the severe losses on the Western Front, battalions of the Royal Scots were amalgamated and the 3/9th became the 4th Reserve with the demise of the military band. Harry and Albert both applied for discharge on the grounds of age quoting 'King's Regs para 392 XXVa'. Albert's discharge was granted on 28 July 1916 at Acreknowe Camp, Hawick where his commanding officer wrote that his military character was 'exemplary' and that he was 'tidy in his habits, hardworking, and of a trustworthy disposition'. His three short months in the army earned him a badge (but no medals) to prove he had served, and this badge would stop the notorious 'white feather' being handed to him in the street.

He quickly returned to show business and a report in *The Scotsman* of 7 November 1916 describes some dramatic and comedy films in the La Scala Picture House in Edinburgh, supplemented by 'Catherine Beaton, contralto and Les Wambas who appear in an attractive musical and gymnastic performance'. He and his daughter seem to have lived in Edinburgh for several months after his army service as they advertised their talents in *The Stage* in October 1917 with an address at 41 Lothian Street in the city. A further *Scotsman* report for 22 January 1918 comments on 'Les Wambas who dabble in music, with cross talk and gymnastics' at the Garrick Theatre, Haymarket, Edinburgh.

By 1918 Albert was 45 years old and his daughter was eighteen. The ethos of entertainment was changing rapidly as the war drew to a close. Music hall was dying, and audiences' preference was now for films. I think Albert tried individually to diversify once again as there are extant three or four adverts in *The Stage* during 1919 and early 1920 for 'Wamba – a smart, clever, juggling, speciality. Contact Bert Wamba in Dorchester, Dorset' but I have no evidence as to any subsequent success or otherwise.

To close this particular chapter in his life, we need to move forward to 11 January 1923 when Mercia married John McCabe in St Patrick's Church, Edinburgh. She was described as a 'restaurant waitress' on the marriage certificate and Albert, her father, was a 'musician'. They were living at 13 Hill Place, a location close to the Empire Theatre (now the Festival Theatre) which continued to provide high-class musical entertainment for the citizens of Edinburgh. Albert was probably living at this stage as a jobbing saxophone/clarinet player. But further changes in his life were in the pipeline, his re-invention of himself continued for several years to come.

ALBERT, ERNEST,
STANLEY AND SYDNEY

T he first part of Albert Dale's career as a professional enter-tainer has been described in the previous chapter. After the marriage of his daughter, Mercia, in 1923 he earned his living as a jobbing musician. It was quite common in the days of silent films for musicians to perform in the pit below the screen to set a scene and add atmosphere . Albert was such a musician, but also kept his options open by forming a small ensemble that played to the patrons of a café in Richmond, Surrey. When the 'talkies' arrived in the late 1920s the days of the cinema musicians were, however, numbered.

But once again, there was a major change in his life when he fell in love with one of the waitresses in the café, Gertrude Herbert. She was of Yorkshire farming stock but she moved to Richmond after her father died. Albert wooed Gertie and they married on 19 November 1925 in Richmond Register Office when he, a widower, was aged 52, and she, a spinster, was aged 23. The 29 year age difference was no real problem, and they lived a full and happy life.

After their marriage, they moved north to York where Gertie, as she was known, had relatives, and they established a theatrical guest house in the Gillygate, not far from the Minster, and close to the Theatre Royal. After spending a fair percentage of his life living in such establishments throughout the country, and knowing the good, the bad and the ugly, I suspect Albert wanted to provide a quality and thoughtful service for their clients. The couple also started a family and they had four children: Alan Stuart Dale born in 1927, Ivor Gordon Dale in 1928, John Kenneth Dale in 1931 and finally Sheila Mercia Dale in 1935. [I found it interesting that his daughter by his first marriage was also called Mercia, very much a Dale family name.]

For some reason that is not very clear, about 1938 or 1939 they upped sticks, opted out of the guest house business, and moved north to Edinburgh, a city that features extensively in my family history. Family lore suggests that Albert's first daughter, Mercia McCabe, living in the Scottish capital, persuaded him to move there as she thought the prospects for work in the city were good. The family settled in a rented house at 14 Pitt Street in the New Town, north of George Street – Pitt Street was later renamed Dundas Street. Albert was 66 when the Second World War started in 1939 and he and his family survived intact.

His eldest son, Alan, married in 1954 in Edinburgh when Albert was 81 and Gertie was fifty-two. The wedding photos show Albert as a cheerful, white-haired elderly man, smartly dressed, with a pleasant smile, and a carefully groomed moustache. His other children all married in due course and various grandchildren arrived. Albert and Gertie left Edinburgh for good about 1958, apparently for financial reasons, and moved for a spell to Bath to

Albert and Gertie Dale in 1954 in Edinburgh at their son Alan's wedding (Dale Collection)

live with their daughter, Sheila, then further south to Portsmouth to stay with their son, John. Albert's first daughter, Mercia McCabe, died of cancer in Edinburgh in 1960 aged 60 and Gertie, his second wife, died in 1964 aged sixty-two. After Gertie's death, Albert moved into a nursing home in Petersfield, Hampshire, where he passed away on the 10 July 1966 aged ninety-three. His death certificate described him as a 'professional musician, retired'. He and Gertie are together again in the Kingston Cemetery, Portsmouth.

There is no doubt he had a full life. He travelled extensively both within the British Isles and further afield, was a talented and versatile musician and entertainer, and adapted his money earning capabilities to suit the circumstances he found himself in. Whether as a clown, musician, gymnast, trapeze artist, juggler, or theatrical guest house owner he gave his all and it is unlikely there are many like him in the modern entertainment business. I never met him but I believe he was a kindly man with a patient temperament. With two wives and two families he extended the Dale family name but the next generation was not quite so involved in the entertainment business.

His first daughter, Mercia, was certainly in show business as I have already demonstrated in the previous chapter, but after her marriage in 1923 she had her own family of a boy and girl (named Mercia, incidentally) to raise and when she died in 1960 she was described as a 'confectioner shop owner'. Being in the retail trade probably gave her a more stable existence with a steady and regular income. She would have witnessed the difficulties her parents had bringing in the money when there were no professional engagements.

None of Albert's second family inherited the professional show business gene with one possible exception. Both Ivor and John became full time Royal Navy men, and both rose to the rank of Chief Petty Officer; John in the submarine branch, Ivor in the Fleet Air Arm. (The genes in their Uncle Ernest must have flowed into them, see below.) They were both gifted amateur musicians and having such a skill in the armed forces would stand them in good stead with their comrades. John, for example, played the violin, cornet and concertina, or squeezebox. There is an apocryphal story that when he served on a RN submarine, there was concern on board as the vessel submerged and a strange wailing noise was heard. The captain brought the vessel back to the surface and the noise disappeared. Submerging again, the noise also started again. A diligent engineer searching the vessel for the cause noticed it seemed to be emanating from the CPO mess. The cause was John's squeezebox which moaned as the pressure changed on submersion, then stopped when the pressure returned to normal on the surface. The comments of the captain have not been recorded!

Sheila married into the RAF Regiment, and Alan was in the Royal Artillery for a while before leaving the Army and changing careers whilst living in Edinburgh. His father-in-law was an established cinema manager so it is no surprise that he decided to go down the same avenue and became the manager of the Ritz Cinema in Rodney Street. About 1958, he moved his family to Glasgow where he rose up the ranks of cinema management until he took over the management of the prime Cinerama complex in Sauchiehall Street – a complex that still exists. Amazingly, this was the location of Cooke's Circus in 1903 when my grandfather directed the orchestra. Life is often a series of cycles, and this was a prominent one in my family. Alan retired in 1988 and died in 1993. He was certainly in the professional entertainment business because of the cinema link, but performing in front of a live audience was not on his agenda.

In a previous paragraph I mentioned the call of the sea for two of Albert's sons. They were not the first of the family to join the Royal Navy, since, that honour goes to Ernest Dale, who was born on 15 January 1877 in Prestwich, Lancashire, the third son and fourth child of the Jester, Henry Thomas Dale. Thanks to the wonder of the internet, the details of Ernest Dale's Royal Navy career are available from the National Archives website. He joined the Navy in 1893 when he was described as a 'labourer', 5'2" tall, light coloured hair, hazel eyes and had a tattoo on his left arm. However, I noticed he added a year to his birth date, making him a year younger than he actually was when he signed on. He was on a training ship for boys for some 18 months in Devonport then was moved to a port guard ship at Pembroke for six months. Thereafter he served for 12 years on various ships and shore stations, all carefully annotated on his individual record sheet, including three years on the *Revenge*, the flag ship of the Mediterranean Fleet. I am not aware he witnessed any shots being fired in anger during his service, but with the First World War looming on the horizon, I am sure he was not too concerned about that. After his discharge on 17 January 1908 at Chatham, where his character was consistently described as: 'Very Good', he was assigned to the Royal Fleet Reserve which required a further commitment of five years. I also noted during his time in the Navy, his height had increased to 5'5".

He returned to Warrington and the 1911 census showed he was living with his father and mother at 16 Ash Grove. He was working as a 'Labourer, Ship Canal' and a few months later he was married, aged 35, on 15 January 1912 – his birthday – to Carrie Counsel, née England, a widow, at the local Register Office. He was described on the marriage certificate as a 'Canal Lock Gateman' while she was 'of independent means' and resided in Heathfield Villa, Stockton Heath. It sounds as if he made a good catch. I noted that in spite of the war starting two years later, there is no evidence he ever served in the armed forces again. It is possible his position on the canal was an exempt occupation, or he may have had a health problem. His wife, Carrie, died aged 40 from 'chronic nephritis' in October 1918 at Barton upon Irwell, Lancashire, and he is described on the certificate as a 'labourer in motor works'. His contribution to the war effort was as a civilian working probably in a munitions factory. I have been unable to trace any surviving children from their marriage.

A search of the Marriage Register in Barton upon Irwell revealed two Ernest Dales got married in the September quarter of 1919. One of these emerged as our man who was described as a 42-year-old widower working as a radiator worker. His new bride was Elizabeth Cookes, a 25-year-old widow, and the marriage took place in the Parish Church of Barton on 12th July 1919. Some further research revealed her maiden name was Elizabeth Wright, and she married Charles Curtis Cookes in 1916. He was serving as a private in the Manchester Regiment when he was killed in action in March 1918. They had a child born in 1917 named Lily Cookes. After Ernest and Elizabeth married, they had three children of their own born in Barton starting with Ernest in 1920, then Eric in 1924 and Grace in 1926.

He is the least known of the Dale brothers and there is little evidence that he had any inclinations towards the entertainment business either in the Navy or after he left. But I am aware that his other four brothers were all taught at least one musical instrument by their father, so there is no reason why he should have been the exception. He died at 77 from cancer in Urmston, Lancashire, in February 1955.

The next son in chronological order was Stanley Henry Dale, born 24 October 1880 at 112 Ridgway Street, Manchester. Like most of the Dale children, he was taught at least one musical instrument when a young lad. However, he did not become a professional musician, preferring the less stressful and more anonymous ranks of the amateur. The 1891 census reveals his occupation as a 'gas stove finisher' but I believe he was actually a journeyman tanner to trade, employed by the Union Tanneries at Howley, near Warrington. His job as a gas stove finisher was a 'fill-in' when work was not available at the tanneries and the company that employed him was the Richmonds, Gas & Stove Company.

On 2 January 1909, aged 28, he married Mary Harper, a 22-year-old Warrington lass, at St James Latchford Parish Church. They had a son, Stanley Albert, later that year followed by another son, Arnold, in 1914. A photograph exists of Warrington Borough Prize Brass Band dated about 1910 or 1911 where the lead cornet player is Stanley H. Dale. He was a member of the band for many years and write-ups about him praise his abilities.

He volunteered for the Royal Field Artillery in 1915 after the war started and seems to have been an excellent soldier as well. Sadly, he was killed in action on 11 June 1917 near Ypres and is buried in Brandhoek Military Cemetery close to Ypres. When he died he was Acting Sergeant Major of 'D' Battery 148th Brigade, RFA. A moving tribute to him was published in *The Warrington Guardian* where his photograph shows a mature man of 36, strong featured, with a firm jaw, and almost steely determination in his eyes. He had dark hair and a fine waxed Kitchener style moustache. I have noted his name on the War Memorial located in Warrington, alongside a long list of other sons of the town who fell in that terrible conflict. His father had died in March 1914, before the war started, but his mother Sarah Ann, must have been devastated to lose one of her sons at a comparatively early age (see p.99).

His widow Mary, known as Polly, was left with two sons, one aged eight, the other aged three so it is no surprise that in 1923, six years later, she married again in Warrington to Thomas Ankers. There were many war widows in Britain at that time and having young children to raise was stressful as well as financially difficult. They had a further boy, named Kenneth Ankers and Thomas

Ankers, Polly's husband, was killed in a motor cycle accident around 1934. Polly herself, died at 80 in 1967.

Both Stanley Albert and Arnold Dale had families whilst domiciled in Warrington. I have met with several members of both these branches, who are second cousins and we all have an interest in our Dale family origins, so we have helped each other by exchanging information, photographs and so on.

The final son was Sydney Edgar Dale, who appeared on 20 December 1890 at the Hop Pole public house, Horsemarket Street, Warrington. As mentioned in a previous chapter, the sound of music would have been in his ears from the day of his birth and Sydney's genes responded accordingly, as he was a professional musician throughout his life. His younger years are a bit vague but he claimed in later life that he started playing professionally from the age of fourteen. A couple of postcards exist sent by him to his brother Stanley, showing he was playing the trombone in circus or

Sydney Edgar Dale seated on left. Ipswich Hippodrome Orchestra, 1911.
(Dale Collection)

Sergeant Stanley Henry Dale, RFA, and his wife Mary about 1917, the year he was killed (Dale Collection)

hippodrome orchestras at an early age. One tattered postcard shows him as a member of a well dressed orchestra playing at the Ipswich Hippodrome around 1911 (see p.98). The 1911 census usefully revealed he was in Lord John Sanger's tenting season orchestra which toured the country for some nine months, and on census night he was performing in Retford, Derbyshire, and being directed by his older brother, Harry Wamba Dale, who was the circus bandmaster. Another card sent from Ohmy's Circus in Chesterfield and dated 26 December 1914 indicates he would be back in

4th Reserve Battalion, Royal Scots about 1918 at Cupar, Fife. Sydney Dale
fourth from right, back row next to nephew Harry Dale, third from right.
Harry's younger brother, Jack Dale, front row, left hand side. (Dale Collection)

Warrington for the New Year. With the First World War in full
swing by this time he waited until 19 February 1916 to marry Eva
Morrison in Middlesbrough then took his brother Harry's advice,
and volunteered for the 3/9 Royal Scots on 29 April 1916, joining up
at Chester. Conscription for married men commenced in May 1916
so by volunteering before this date, I think he was able to enlist in
the regiment he preferred. As I have indicated elsewhere, five Dale
family members eventually joined the same Scottish battalion. In
December 1916, his wife Eva produced a child named Sarah who
was born in Middlesbrough.

I have an interesting photo of Sydney taken while he was
serving in the army (see above). It shows the 4th (Reserve)
Battalion, Royal Scots taken about 1919 in Cupar, Fife, with Sydney
in the back row clutching his trombone standing beside my dad's
older brother, Syd's nephew, yet another Harry Dale. This Harry
Dale became a virtuoso on the trombone and I have no doubt he
got some tips from his Uncle Syd whilst they served together. In the
front row left is another nephew, John (Jack) Dale, whose instrumental prowess was on the saxophone/ clarinet.

Sydney's Army service papers survived the London Blitz during
the Second World War, but only just, forming part of what is
known as the 'Burnt Documents'. They reveal that on joining he

Sydney Dale aged
70 on his third
honeymoon in
London, 1960
(Dale Collection)

was 5'3" tall, only 7 stone 8 pounds in weight and his physical development was 'fair', being classed BII. He never fired a shot in anger
and served until the end of the war, being demobbed at Cupar on
18 February 1919. He returned to Middlesbrough where his wife was
living at Gilkes Street.

His subsequent career is a bit of a mystery though family lore
had him playing 'big band' music in the thirties, forties and fifties
under band-leaders apparently including Jack Payne, Jack Parnell
and Billy Cotton. I have never managed to find real evidence of this
but any experts in the music world who can find the name of
trombonist Sydney Edgar Dale (or Sydney Edgar, as I believe he
was also known) amongst band members might let me know!

I do know he married three times, perhaps an occupational hazard of touring musicians, his last wife being his landlady in Coventry, Rose Butlin, whom he married at 70 in 1960, when he was aged 70 (see previous page). The photo of Sydney on his honeymoon in London, shows the same enigmatic smile dancing on his lips that appears in other photos. He was a popular member of the Dale family and figures in a number of family 'snaps' at various times and locations. He died in 1984 aged 94 in Coventry where the local paper wrote a piece about 'the former trombonist at Coventry Theatre Orchestra'. The paragraph states that 'he was born into a theatrical family and first appeared on the stage as a child, but played the trombone professionally from the age of 14'. 'After many years on tour with various bands, he settled in Coventry in 1956, retiring in 1963' when he would have been 73 years old. I suspect Sydney enjoyed life and music was his religion.

I have, on occasion, imagined a celestial orchestra with the Dale brothers and their father providing two cornets, a saxophone, a trombone and a concertina as first choice instruments, but doubling on a range of others including the violin, tubular bells, banjo, piano, handbells and musical glasses. This family orchestra would have been impressive, but wait until you read about the talented Dale sisters, and the additional contribution they could have made to this musical mélange!

HARRY WAMBA –
GRANDFATHER DALE

My grandfather Harry Dale, the third child and second son of Harry and Sarah Ann Dale, was born at 19 Eden Street, Oldham on 26 January 1875. As usual, I have no specific details of his early childhood but he did have a propensity for, and love of music, no doubt fostered by his talented father. The first official document that mentions him is the 1881 census where the Dale family were living at Ridgway Street, Manchester, and he was aged six and a scholar. There is a story that at about 13 he had a major argument with a music teacher at his school, claiming he knew more about a particular musical situation than the teacher. After a discussion with his father, who was sympathetic to his son's argument, the young Harry never went back to school again. As a result, his father got him a position in the orchestra at the Bellevue Gardens in Manchester. I have found printed evidence of his prowess on the cornet when his father ran the Hop Pole Concert Hall in Warrington in 1890. Young Harry performed as a solo cornettist aged 15 and had a mention in *The Era* for 5 April of that year alongside his sister Amy and his father. The 1891 census shows him as a 'bar tender', aged 16, in the Victoria Hotel, Stockport, the proprietor at that time being his father. He then seems to have joined the orchestra of an ocean liner that sailed to Australia and back a few times before he returned permanently to Britain and sought out a means of livelihood. No doubt all this early experience would have endowed him with confidence in his own abilities as well as showing him a bit of the Empire, and how other professional musicians made a living.

In Chapter 7 I have already outlined his early career as a musical clown working alongside his older brother Albert when they formed the Brothers Wamba. I also drew attention to the variety of instruments on which they performed, and which they were proud to advertise in publications such as *The Era* and *The Stage*.

My personal view is that Harry Dale had a yen to conduct a

circus orchestra from early on in his career. Cooke's Circus appearing in Arbroath and Perth in the autumn of 1897 had him as orchestral director as well as appearing in the ring with his brother performing their 'Brothers Wamba' act. The years 1898 and 1899 saw them in various circuses throughout Britain with their act; and a clipping from *The Era* of 11 November 1899 mentions the opening of Cooke's Circus in Edinburgh for the season with 'a fine selection by the band under Mr Harry Wamba, a clever cornettist as well as conductor'. The tour of South Africa with Bonamici's International Circus starting in late 1900 was a milestone in their career, but thereafter they had difficulty in getting consistent bookings. Perhaps dropping out of the bookings radar for nearly a year was the penalty they paid.

Summarising his private life, he married Jane, or Jeannie, Lavin on 15 February 1899 in Edinburgh two days after the end of John Henry Cooke's circus season. I have no idea how they first met but it may be that the Lavins took in theatrical guests at their house, No. 36 Grassmarket, also known as Dunlop's Court, which was close to Cooke's Circus at East Fountainbridge. (Dunlop's Court still exists, although some modernisation has taken place.) Their

Harry Wamba Dale holding cornet and baton, with circus orchestra; possibly Edinburgh about 1902 or 1903 (Dale Collection)

Programme for Cooke's
Royal Circus, Edinburgh,
December 1906
(Dale Collection)

first child, a girl, was born in January 1900, but she died 11 hours later. The death certificate describes the cause as 'inanition' which the dictionary defines as 'exhaustion through lack of food'. As far as I know, the baby was never named but it must have been a major blow to the newly weds. The next child was born on 17 March 1901, still at 36 Grassmarket, and was a boy named, inevitably, 'Harry'. Young Harry was baptised on 12 April in St Columba's-by-the-Castle, a Scottish Episcopalian Church that still exists in Johnston Terrace just below Edinburgh Castle.

The 1901 census shows Jeannie Dale and her son, Harry, staying at 36 Grassmarket with her parents. [Harry Wamba Dale was abroad, performing with his brother Albert in South Africa so did not appear in this particular census.] The next family member to arrive was John Lavin Dale, in later life always known as 'Jack', born on 23 January 1903, also at 36 Grassmarket, and also baptised in St Columba's on 20 February. The two-year pattern continued with a third boy born on 11 February 1905 in the same location, and baptised Charles William Dale in the same church on 24 March. The little boy died on 9 March 1907 from measles and pneumonia aged two. The last member of this particular family was the most important as far as I am concerned, as it was my father, born on 30 April 1908 at Leaside Cottage, Viewforth, Edinburgh, and named after three of his father's brothers – Albert Stanley Ernest Dale. Dad was baptised on 31 May at St Kentigern's Chapel in St Peter's Place, near Viewforth, also a Scottish Episcopalian Chapel. The shell of this little church still exists but it is in a sad rundown condition. It was a Mission Chapel originally established by the grand St John's Episcopalian Church at the West End of Princes Street, and a prominent Edinburgh landmark. My dad hated all his Christian names but settled eventually for 'Albert,' reduced even further to 'Bert'.

When Harry and Albert Dale decided to dissolve their brothers' act around 1902, Albert remained as a stage artist, but Harry took the musical route. His decision was to operate 'behind the scenes' as a musical director. There is plenty of evidence that he recruited musicians for the orchestras he led, arranged the music, composed music, rehearsed the orchestras, and delivered good music for any occasion. As well as his musical talent, he needed to be a good man manager and have a feel for the occasion, whether it was a circus act, or an overture to introduce a show. As with all professionals, up

Harry Wamba and Jeannie Lavin Dale with their three sons: Jack at back, Harry in front, Albert (Bert) on his mother's knee, 1908 (Dale Collection)

to the outbreak of the First World War, his next engagement relied on his reputation, his contacts and the references he got from his patrons. There is no doubt in my mind that his father helped him get established and his father's links with John Henry Cooke, the circus proprietor, opened the door for the many years he worked with Cooke from about 1897 to Cooke's eventual retirement in 1911.

I have been fortunate in obtaining a few examples of programmes from Cooke's Circus seasons where my grandfather was part of the first act usually billed 'Overture by the Orchestra'. The National Archives for Scotland hold three or four examples, the Central Library in Edinburgh is another source, and a friend of mine provided a beautiful original full colour programme dated 29 December 1906 from a contact in London (see p.105). Curiously, one programme from 1903 gave Harry Wamba the title of Professor, while a 1910 version designates him as Lieutenant H. Wamba. Why he chose such titles is not known, but mostly he was just 'Conductor – Harry Wamba'. The 1906 programme mentioned above also recognised his composing talent by indicating he wrote the music for the 'Ally Sloper's Big Water Carnival', a pantomime extravaganza based on a cartoon character, produced by Cooke over the Christmas weeks.

His need to gather together a suitable orchestra before the start of each season is easily followed in the trade newspapers where adverts under the heading 'Musicians Wanted' spelt out in detail the instrumentalists required, for how long, and at what salary. An example from *The Era* of 13 November 1909 states:

> JOHN HENRY COOKE'S ROYAL CIRCUS, Edinburgh Wanted – musicians for orchestra for above establishment. Must be thoroughly used to circus and variety. AMU's preferred. Opening date 27th November. Applications to Harry Wamba, Leeside, Viewforth Square, Edinburgh.

Two things struck me about this advert. Firstly, the short time scale; advertising his requirements only two weeks before the first night and, secondly, the demand that the musicians had to be AMUs. The AMU was the Amalgamated Musicians Union so presumably membership meant they were professionals and experienced [there was also a contemporary rival entitled the 'National Federation of Professional Musicians', but my researches indicated that AMU members seemed to be preferred in most adverts seeking musicians]. However, although the circus did open on 27 November, a further advert appeared in the same publication on 4 December stating:

> JOHN HENRY COOKE'S ROYAL CIRCUS, Edinburgh
> Wanted at once, good first violin, viola and first cornet.
> Terms 35s for six evening performances and two matinees.
> Professional AMUs, not amateurs.
> Wire to Harry Wamba, Musical Director.

There is a slight feeling of desperation in this advert as three vital players were required either as new orchestra members, or replacements for 'amateurs' or individuals not 'used to circus and variety'. There were no further adverts so presumably the crisis was resolved and suitable men – always men – were found.

I have a curious photograph of my grandfather as a conductor with an orchestra dressed to the full in their white ties and tails, sitting with their instruments looking seriously at the camera (see p.104). Curious because the background is not a studio or even a circus interior, but seems to be a back garden or yard somewhere. The date is around the early 1900s judging by the hairstyles, moustaches and clothing of the gentlemen concerned. A dress rehearsal, perhaps, but outside?

John Henry Cooke retired from his circus business in 1911 aged 74 and sold the Royal Circus in East Fountainbridge to a local cinema operator called R.C. Buchanan. The competition from the film industry was intense and the music halls and circuses were now suffering from this popular new technology. Latterly, Cooke had been showing films to his audiences but the design of a circus ring is not ideal for such a show. There is a story that patrons in the expensive seats could see the film the proper way round, but those in the cheap seats who sat on the opposite side of the screen, saw the film projected the wrong way round! The Royal Circus building, a landmark in Edinburgh, was altered and became a cinema in early 1911 and remained as such until about 1932 when it was internally altered again and became a variety theatre named The Palladium. It was quite small, with about a thousand seats, and was often called the 'University of Music Halls' as many future stars graduated from its stage. Its days were numbered when television came along so the original building was closed in 1968, had a brief period as a dance club and was finally demolished in 1984. A block of residential flats now occupies the site, and there is no sign anywhere nearby, to Edinburgh's shame, indicating this was once the location of a very popular circus and variety theatre (see p.2).

Cooke's retiral affected grandfather Dale immediately. After 14 years of comfortable success he needed to find other means of earning a living to support his wife and three boys. An advert appeared in the 'Musicians Wanted' column of *The Era* dated 28 January 1911:

LORD JOHN SANGER & SONS LTD
Tented Season 1911

Wanted: first violin and viola, both to play either first or second cornet or E flat horn for Parade. Also wanted, clarinet, second cornet to play first cornet on Parade. Double drummer with effects, bass drum provided. Must be strong players and experienced in other instruments. 32s 6d. Two references (copies only) must be forwarded with application to Harry Wamba, Musical Director, Leeside House, Viewforth Square, Edinburgh.

This is quite a detailed advert laying down complex conditions for the musicians and looking for some interesting combinations – a violinist who doubled on a cornet, for example. The tented circus of 'Lord John Sanger' was a popular spectacle throughout Britain, and the parade of performers and animals was an essential feature of the marketing plan to get paying customers through the door.

Another advert followed on 11 February in the same publication raising the terms to 35 shillings a week for a 'First violinist to combine either cornet, horn or baritone'. Knowing that my grandfather was skilled on a number of instruments – including violin and cornet – perhaps made him think it was a common combination and therefore easy to get suitable applicants.

The tented season commenced in March in the south of England. The 1911 census held on 2 of April, revealed Harry Wamba Dale living in a boarding house with other musicians in the town of Retford in Derbyshire. I was then surprised, and delighted, to find that his younger brother, Sydney Edgar Dale, was also boarding in Retford, but at a different address, and was part of a circus band. I can only assume he was also in Lord John Sanger's Circus Orchestra, and was being directed by his elder brother.

A further advert in *The Era* on 1 April sought a 'good viola must play brass instrument on Parade'. Applicants were invited to write to Harry Wamba at Burstow Lodge, Horley, Surrey.

Throughout 1911 regular adverts appeared seeking different musical skills especially a 'double drummer with effects' and these adverts showed me the progress of Lord John's circus as it wound its way northwards through the spring and summer. Chester-Le-Street, Sunderland, Bedlington, Ashington then across the Scottish border to Hawick in May, Edinburgh, Bathgate, Crieff, and Blairgowrie in June, Inverbervie, Montrose, Dundee and Kinross in July, then Kilmarnock, Irvine and Largs in August revealed an exhausting schedule for all concerned – human and animal – as the circus was often only one day in a small location and two or three days in the larger towns and cities.

A report for the Dundee appearance is given under the heading 'Showman's World' in *The Era* for 22 July 1911:

LORD JOHN SANGER'S ROYAL HIPPODROME & MENAGERIE in Dundee

The above show paid a successful visit to Dundee on Friday & Saturday 14 & 15 July. A huge tent pitched on the west end of the esplanade drew large crowds both at the afternoon and evening performances. Every item on the programme was of a high class with Coleman & Co's three elephants, Sanger's performing sea lions, the Austin bare back horse riders, the acrobatic Dundas Troupe, the capital clown Pimpo, and the Three Sydneys on the wire. The band, under the direction of Mr Harry Wamba, played appropriate music.

I have to assume his problems with violinists, cornettists and a double drummer had been resolved, at least temporarily. It is worth mentioning that 'Pimpo', the equestrian clown, was the eldest son of Lord John Sanger, and was named Herbert Sanger.

A further report appeared on 19 August when the circus was in Kilmarnock. The commentary stated: 'Lord John Sanger's Circus visited this town on Monday and gave a couple of very successful performances. The midday parade was witnessed by thousands of people.'

Moving around the country with a tented circus was a new experience for Harry Wamba Dale. As far as I am aware he had never done it before, but he did repeat the exercise so perhaps the tiring schedule was compensated for by the money he earned. Most of the adverts for musicians offered 32 shillings and sixpence, in old money, for a week's work. In our current currency that would be £1.62.5 which seems rather little, but in comparison with other advertisements of the period, Sanger's were offering a high end of the market salary. Harry Wamba Dale, as musical director, was probably earning between £2 and £2.50 per week. It must have been a tiring year.

Sanger's Circus continued its merry way down the east coast of England with stops in Hexham and Newcastle in September and concluded sometime in late October or early November. After a rest in Edinburgh, my grandfather started all over again as an advert appeared on 2 December in *The Era* which showed:

CURZON HALL, Birmingham
To open December 26th
Wanted for E.H. Bostock's Circus Season an orchestra of ten sight reading musicians. Those with circus experience preferred. Good orchestral pianist or harpist, write. Two performances daily. Lowest terms in first letter. No fancy salaries. Two references (copies). Applications to Harry Wamba, Musical Director, Leeside, Viewforth Square, Edinburgh.
Those with me during the summer, if at liberty, write. Also, J.H. Dickman, violinist.

He never left much time for applications but the system seemed to work. Mr Dickman, the violinist, perhaps doubled on the cornet or other brass instrument, hence his popularity! After the show opened on 26 December, he advertised again in *The Era* on 30 December for a 'clarinet, must be used to circus business' and after that his orchestra of 10 sight reading musicians seemed to perform to his exacting standard. A couple of reports in *The Era* for January stated: 'Bostock's Circus is a popular place of entertainment. The programme is crammed with first rate attractions …' and 'the circus retains its popularity with "Texas", the spectacular water drama produced last week has become one of the biggest features of the local amusement world …'

The Birmingham indoor season was comparatively short and probably finished in early February as once again he launched his recruitment drive on 17 February 1912 in *The Era* in the 'Musicians Wanted' column seeking 'experienced musicians' for Lord John Sanger's 1912 Tenting Season. The tour started in the London area on 18 March.

Domestically, the family had moved to a different rented house at 10 Hailes Street, off Gilmore Place. This location was only three minutes' walk from the King's Theatre in Leven Street, a fine Edwardian variety theatre opened in 1906 which is a favourite, even today, with Edinburgh audiences. I believe he became a member of the pit orchestra there from time to time, but not the musical director, and he also performed in the Theatre Royal at the top of Leith Walk, another popular variety theatre, long since gone. His ability on several instruments was probably a useful asset. He is also known to have supplemented his income from time to time by acting as a barman in one or two Edinburgh public houses – a trade he had learnt many years before in the Victoria Hotel, Stockport.

There seems to have been a short but unusual interlude in his life in 1913. His older brother, Albert, lost his wife in September 1912 in Sumatra from malaria whilst performing with a circus there, as described in Chapter 7. On returning to Britain, Albert had to earn a living and I was surprised to find an advert in *The Era* for April 1913 showing the re-formation of the 'Brothers Wamba' musical act. They performed 'a musical novelty act' a couple of times in the west of Scotland at Clydebank and Glasgow, then disappeared again. A further act was advertised on the 23 July for 'The Three Dales in their refined artistic musical and vocal act' who again performed a couple of times, but disappeared once more. I can only conjecture that Harry Wamba Dale was trying to get his brother's shattered confidence back together again but was struggling to get results. I have not found any further evidence for this period of his life, but I have a certain admiration for him as he had a good relationship with the Sanger Circus organisation and probably could have gone with them for a further tented season. Instead he chose to go back on the stage with his brother. During this period his wife, Jeannie

Dale, ran a series of advertisements in *The Era* in late 1913 and early 1914 under the 'Professional Apartments' column, seeking boarders for their house at 10 Hailes Street, 'only two minutes from the "Kings" (Theatre)'.

I think Harry Wamba Dale maintained this existence for several more months, probably supplemented by playing in theatre orchestras until the Great War started on 4 August 1914. He volunteered in 1915.

His army papers survived and gave me some additional information about him. He was a volunteer and his attestation took place in Edinburgh on 11 August 1915 at the East Claremont Drill Hall of the 3/9th Battalion, Royal Scots, a territorial battalion. (This drill hall is still used by the army.) He signed himself as 'Harry Wamba Dale' and his family address was now 10 Lauriston Park, close to Tollcross in the city. The medical report showed him to be 5'4" tall, with brown eyes and hair and he was passed fit by the medical officer but the downside was his age. He was 40 years 6 months old when he joined. The Royal Scots, named the 1st Regiment of Foot, was the oldest line regiment of the British Army and was often labelled 'Pontius Pilate's Bodyguard' with a proud history going back to 1633. It had the accolade of 'The Lothian Regiment' and as such, wore tartan trews when on parade. However, the 9th Battalion had the unique addendum of being labelled 'Highland', and these Royal Scots wore the kilt, in particular the stylish green tartan of Hunting Stewart. The Edinburgh folk were fond of this battalion which they called 'the Dandy Ninth' as the soldiers were always smartly turned out. He was assigned to the battalion military band – not the pipes and drums – under Band Sergeant Dan Sweeney. Harry Wamba Dale was promoted band lance corporal a month after enrolment, then up to band corporal in November 1915. There is a fine photograph (see p.136) of the band taken at Stobs Camp in the Borders where he sits in the front row holding a cornet next to Sergeant Sweeney, with the tartan clad military musicians looking proudly at the camera. The Dandy Ninth proved a useful battalion for the Dales as other family members joined in due course. His older brother Albert Dale volunteered on 25 April 1916 while younger brother, Sydney, a virtuoso trombonist, volunteered on 29 April 1916. Finally, two of Harry Wamba Dale's sons: young Harry, aged 15, volunteered in October 1916, and Jack, aged 14, also wore the Royal

Scots uniform after 1917. With five Dales in the Royal Scots the Kaiser must have known his days were numbered.

I think Harry Wamba Dale was quite clever in volunteering for the Army when he did, and presumably he encouraged his two brothers to do so as well. Lord Kitchener, then followed by the Earl of Derby, had tried hard to get more volunteers to join during 1915 but the slaughter on the Western Front in particular had created more demand for soldiers than the volunteer system could provide. As a result, the government passed the Military Service Act in January 1916 conscripting all unmarried men between the ages of 18 and 41. A second Act passed in May the same year called up married men. The three Dale brothers were together in the military band as volunteers before these Acts were implemented. [The other Dale brother in the Army, Stanley Henry, also volunteered, but in a previous chapter I have mentioned his death on the Western Front in 1917 whilst serving with the Royal Field Artillery.]

Harry Wamba Dale was not very long in uniform. On 15 July 1916 he wrote to his commanding officer, Captain F.R. Lucas that 'as the band of the 3/9 Royal Scots has been disbanded, I beg to claim a discharge under Army Council Instruction 1219 Para 5 when my age on 26th July 1916 will be 41 years 6 months'. Due to the heavy losses on the front, the 3/9th Battalion and the 4th Reserve Battalion of the Royal Scots were amalgamated in July resulting in the loss of the military band. Older brother Albert sent an identical letter on the same date and both brothers were granted their discharge on 28 July 1916. Harry had served King and Country for slightly less than a year; Albert for three months. They were both granted a badge to wear indicating they had been in the Army thus avoiding the embarrassment of being given a white feather on the street by so-called patriotic ladies.

On his discharge, he did not return to the family home but briefly stayed in Edinburgh with his brother at lodgings in Lothian Street. There had been family tensions for some time and after his enrolment into the army, Jeannie, his wife, had found it difficult to look after the three boys. The two older boys joined the Army leaving my dad, Bert, on his own. Sadly, Jeannie took to the bottle, and Dad had to put up with some difficult behaviour. He ran away from home as I will relate in a later chapter. Harry Wamba Dale also decided he had had enough of domestic life. He left Edinburgh never to return and moved to London seeking work.

He sought musical work in London but did not have any great success. I have, however, noted a couple of entries in *The Stage* dated March 1919 where he worked at the Hippodrome, Stoke on Trent, then the Tivoli Theatre at New Brighton. In the latter case, the entertainment was a review named 'The Scots Brigade' described as 'wholesome entertainment with the orchestra and chorus under the capable direction of Harry Wamba'.

I have been told that work for jobbing musicians was hard to find at this time but whilst in London, he answered an advertisement for a position in a theatre orchestra in West Hartlepool, scraped enough money together to buy a train ticket there for an interview, and eventually got the job. He settled in the town in 1920 and lived there for the rest of his life. The theatre where he worked became a cinema and he lost his position once more. He took a pragmatic approach and started a window cleaning business in the town which was modestly successful. He was closely involved with the Hartlepool Military Band where he was the musical director, leading the band on appropriate occasions such as the annual Armistice Day parade. He was mentioned in the local *Northern Daily Mail* of 13th November 1933 at the Co-operative Society Armistice commemoration where the paper reported the 'Last Post was sounded by Mr Harry Wamba Dale, and the company stood to attention during a minute's silence'. An excellent photograph (see opposite) also shows him amongst his ex-army comrades at a dinner holding his cornet and looking as dapper as always.

I also possess a neat and skilful watercolour which he painted of a sailing vessel on the sea. Dad told me his father was a good drawer and painter but virtually everything was related to seascapes. Was this a restless spirit at work? Did he long for better things in other places and painting was his release? I will never know, but I believe he produced quite a number of these paintings some of which were given away, or even sold, so anyone with an original 'H. Dale' is invited to contact me!

As far as I know from my father and his brothers, there was little contact between them and their father, although odd visits took place as I have a photograph of my parents in 1934 standing smiling with Harry Wamba Dale in Hartlepool. Dad married in 1937 and that was the same year his mother, Jeannie Lavin Dale, died from cancer in Edinburgh. I only met my grandfather once, in September 1947 when I was eight years old. We all travelled to

Hartlepool with Jeannie Lavin Dale's elder sister to try and effect some form of reconciliation but sadly it never happened. I do remember a small, white-haired dapper man with a fine waxed moustache who patted me on the head but that is all. Harry Wamba Dale died on 20 June 1957 aged 82 from heart complications and is buried in Hartlepool. He was described on the death certificate as a 'retired professional musician' – a musician is all he ever was, and ever wanted to be.

The First World War was a significant milestone in the life of the country, as it changed so many attitudes and expectations, and when the fighting finished, there was no return to the cosy and

Harry Wamba Dale with cornet. Remembrance Day 1933 in Hartlepool. (Dale Collection)

familiar times of Edwardian Britain, especially in the entertainment profession. Harry Wamba Dale had to re-invent himself, but that characteristic was a feature of most of my Dale ancestors.

I regret never having had more contact with him as I grew older but only when I launched my family research did I find out about his story, and how it affected my father and his brothers. I have a close and loving family of my own so I find it difficult to understand how families can divide and split when life is so short and we cannot change what has happened in the past. Tolerance and forgiveness are essential ingredients in a family, but, sadly, there are too many examples of the exact opposite that create much unhappiness.

THE DAUGHTERS OF MR HARRY DALE

As well as having five sons, Harry and Sarah Ann Dale produced an equal number of daughters who survived childbirth. They had a further daughter, Frances Leah Dale in 1884 but she died aged six months in 1885. In chronological order the survivors were: Amy b.1872, Ella b.1878, Lottie b.1883, Vera Maud b.1889 and finally Doris May b.1893. Four of them were in the professional entertainment business for a period, but marriage changed the direction of their lives, and as far as I know, none of them resumed being entertainers thereafter.

Amy was born in London when Harry Dale was performing in the London music halls. Her full name was Amy Mary Ann Dale and I assume she was named after her paternal grandmother, Mary Ann Dale/Claridge/Corrock. I have searched long and hard but have been unable to find a birth certificate for Amy Dale anywhere in London, Middlesex or other outlying districts. Although birth registration had been in place in England since 1837, it was not a compulsory requirement until 1875 so several births slipped through the net and it seems Amy's birth was one of them. The next step would be to find her baptism but again, I have had no success. With hundreds of churches in London and the environs, there is probably an entry somewhere, but so far I have failed to find it. There is, however, other evidence about her birth found in the census returns as well as her own marriage and death certificates in later life but no specific birth date is given, only confirmation of the year.

I have no information about her early life but there is evidence in the entertainment press that she was taking part in show business from about age fourteen. There is an advert in *The Era* dated 8 May 1886 where her name appears amongst those performing in 'Rolland's New Iron Circus' in Jersey opening on the 24 May. Her father, Harry Dale, is also listed, as the 'Prince of Jesters'. There are a couple of reports about the circus in Jersey but there is no mention of Amy, or the act in which she was involved.

The next references to her are more specific as she was included in the company performing at the Hop Pole Concert Hall, Warrington, where her father was the proprietor, from April 1890 to about March 1891 and she was described as a 'contralto'. She was obviously musical, as the 1891 census return for the Dale family in Stockport describes her as a 'professional pianist'. Beyond this minimal information, I have been unable to find any more details about her. Confirmed photos exist of the other daughters of Harry Dale but none exist of her.

On 9 June 1895 she was married, aged 23, in St Paul's Parish Church, Warrington, to Richard Bailey, a self-employed earthenware dealer. The 1901 census showed that the couple were living in Forster Street, Warrington and had a son named Arnold, born in 1897, a daughter named May born in 1899, while the 1911 census showed two further children: Amy born in 1902, then Edna in June 1905. Tragically, Amy Bailey née Dale died in Runcorn, aged 33 on 21 July 1905 a short time after her last child was born, from heart and septicaemia problems. Her husband, Richard, was left with four young children to raise, so it is no surprise that he married again in 1909. Thereafter, he moved from Warrington to Stockton Heath, near Runcorn.

The second daughter, Ella Dale, was born on 29 December 1878 at 11 Lawson Street, Sunderland, Co. Durham. Her father, Harry Dale, was performing at the Wear Music Hall, Sunderland for a few weeks over Christmas and New Year, and his wife seemed to follow him around at this stage in spite of having two sons and a daughter already [the landlady at the theatrical digs must have been quite understanding to have a pregnant mother and three young children as guests]. Ella's early life, as with most of my ancestors, is unknown but there is no doubt she was taught music by her father, and possibly her mother, and was known to be a competent pianist as well as a singer, dancer and performer on various other instruments. She was one of the three Dale sisters who formed the Parez Sisters, a musical act that toured the music halls and circuses in the Edwardian period.

The third daughter and seventh child was Lottie Dale, christened as such, and not Charlotte as might be expected. She was born on 29 April 1883 at 1 Broadfield Park Square, Ecclesall, near Sheffield, Yorkshire, where her father was once more performing.

Again, she received a good grounding in music from her parents, and latterly was known as a very good singer and instrumentalist. She was the second member of the Parez Sisters.

The fifth daughter and ninth child in the Dale family was born Vera Maud Dale on 29 January 1889 in the village of Bradford, near Prestwich, now located in north west Manchester. She was physically quite small, taking after her mother, Sarah Ann, who was less than five feet tall. Vera Maud was known to the family and friends as 'Dot'. In my early research on the family, I was thrown by this, thinking there was a daughter named 'Dorothy' whom I could never find in the official documentation. However, explanatory evidence came from a couple of sources and latterly a confirmed photograph of her turned up where she had signed herself as 'Dot'. This is one of the hazards of family research, where a pet name can be accepted as the given name, and the researcher is led off on the

Lottie Dale, the middle sister of the Parez Trio, 1909 (Dale Collection)

Vera Maud Dale, the youngest of the Parez Trio. Date unknown.
(Dale Collection)

wrong track. My own mother was known as 'Cis' all her life but was christened Margaret Malcolm Nelson and was only addressed formally as 'Margaret' in the last year or two of her life when in a nursing home. Vera Maud Dale was the third member of the Parez Sisters.

The sixth daughter and final child to be born in the family was Doris May Dale born in Warrington, Lancashire, on 26 July 1893 at 10 Orford Avenue. As far as I know, she did not follow the musical trail but chose a more domestic existence.

The official census details for 1881 show Harry Dale and his family living at 112 Ridgeway Street, Manchester with Amy, aged nine, listed as a scholar, and Ella aged two. Moving on ten years to 1891, they are domiciled in the Victoria Hotel, Stockport in Cheshire, where Amy aged 19 is a 'professional pianist', and Ella, aged 12 and Lottie aged seven are scholars while Vera Maud is aged two. The next census in 1901 where the family are living at 32 Mill Lane, Warrington, is more revealing. Ella, aged 22, Lottie aged 17 and Vera Maud aged 12, are all listed as being a 'professional musician'. The baby of the family, Doris, is aged seven and a scholar. I am surprised at Vera Maud, aged 12, being a wage earner but that is what the census entry says.

The three 'professional musicians' were starting their career as the Parez Sisters, sometimes known as the Parez Trio. Where the name 'Parez' came from is not known, but it does have a continental sound to it which may have been important. I suspect the two older girls, Ella and Lottie, may have performed as musicians before the launch of the Parez Sisters but I have no documentary evidence to support this.

The earliest tangible reference found is dated 21 February 1901 and is a two-line advert in *The Stage* that says simply:

THREE SISTERS PAREZ, *High Class Musical Act.*
Circus, Great Grimsby.

The Era of 16 March 1901 reporting on Dent's Grand Circus in Great Grimsby commented '… the Three Sisters Parez gave a musical entertainment which is highly appreciated'. It will not be a surprise to readers that their father, Harry Dale, was also performing at this circus as 'the musical jester'. There is a lot of circumstantial evidence over the years that Harry Dale nourished his family in their early days on the stage and in the circus arena.

Their appearances in 1901 seem to have been a bit patchy as in the spring and early summer they were advertising their act. I have not found any reports. By September they were at the Hippodrome in Brighton alongside their father once again, then they had a week at the Paddington Palace in Liverpool followed by the month of November at North Shields Borough Circus where the general manager just happened to be a Mr H. Dale. Across the Border to Glasgow at Bostock's Zoo Circus then followed in December with a return to the North Shields Circus in January 1902. There was praise for their act which was described as a 'high class musical melange and expert hand bell players'.

The use of hand bells seems to have been a Dale family speciality. There is evidence of Harry Dale introducing it to his act several years before, whilst his two sons, the Brothers Wamba, were also skilled exponents. The Parez Sisters followed on as their act grew in confidence and by the late summer of 1902 they were calling themselves 'Champion Hand Bell Ringers' in *The Era* of 13 September. They performed at Ohmy's Circus in Preston, then

King's in Wigan with a diversion to 'Tomkinson's Royal Choir' in November with a spell at Ohmy's back in Wigan over the Christmas period. They now marketed themselves as '... a beautiful musical act, hand bell marvels and graceful dancers'. Their mother was originally a dancer, so she may have coached them.

The *Southport Visitor* reported on the 6 January 1903: 'Pleasing variety offered by the Parez Trio in their musical act in which they show wonderful skill on some novel instruments.' *The Northern Daily Mail* of 13 January 1903 gave an effusive description: 'The Parez Trio also pleased their hearers with their selections on a variety of musical instruments. Perhaps one of the most effective items was the solo on the glasses of water, the sweetest of music being produced.'

Later in the year they appeared in a variety of locations such as the Princess Theatre in Horwich, near Bolton, and in Hull where Lottie Dale was given a special mention in *The Stage* of 24 September for her singing. A return to Hull in November at the Hippodrome, then in December at the Empire Theatre, found Harry Dale once again on the billing while Lottie, now renamed 'Lottie Wamba' 'wins notice as a vocalist' whilst the Parez Trio 'is enjoyed'.

Then 1904 arrived and the girls set off on a grand pantomime tour of Wales. They seem to have shaken off the attentions of their father by now and presumably were confident enough to stand on their own feet at last. They started off at Carmarthen Assembly Halls in the west of Wales in the pantomime 'Dick Whittington and His Cat' produced by the Hopkins Brothers and their act 'met with appreciation'. Hopkins then took the pantomime to the Assembly Halls in Monmouth for a week, followed by the Public Hall in Tredegar.

After a brief period euphemistically called 'disengagement' they were back in the circus arena again at Chesterfield in Algie's Hippodrome in early March. Carlisle followed with a return to Chesterfield with Ohmy's Circus this time in May. Late May 1904 was spent at the Empire Music Hall in Wrexham, then the Hippodrome in Leigh while Carmarthen beckoned again in early June. They then crossed the Irish Sea to Dublin to join every beer drinker's dream, the Guinness Fete in mid-June, which was held in the Royal Society Grounds.

An advert appeared in *The Era* of 2 July 1904 as follows:

PAREZ TRIO (Ladies)
Great Musical Act
Bagpipes, Handbells and £100 worth of instruments.
Perm. 32 Mill Lane,
Warrington.

As a passionate Scot, I was delighted to see that my ancestors had embraced the most iconic of instruments, but not necessarily the easiest to learn and play. No doubt performing to essentially English or Welsh audiences would have been a challenge but they would have had no problems in Scotland or Ireland although the purists might have expressed some criticism. Perhaps they were ahead of the pack in popularising the pipes all these years ago, which over the past few years of this century have appeared in all guises from serious pibroch – the classical music of the bagpipe – to modern hit tunes emanating from the military as well as the pop music genre.

The £100 of instruments is also enlightening as such a sum was large by Edwardian standards where a wage of £1 a week was not uncommon. The figure was probably exaggerated and the purchases might have been second-hand rather than spanking new. Nevertheless, it was a good marketing ploy designed to attract the theatre managers and agents who booked the acts.

Steady employment followed this advert as I found them in Wolverhampton in early August, then Manchester for three weeks at different venues – the Hippodrome, Queens Park Hippodrome and the Metropole. However, it is worth noting that the manager of the Metropole, Mr W.B. Broadhead also managed the other two theatres as well, so he probably got good discount value from the Parez Trio contract! Salford, Sheffield, Rochdale, Middleton and Pontefract then received a visit proving the popularity of the northern music halls for Harry Dale's daughters as the end of 1904 beckoned.

The New Year had the girls in Liverpool for a week at the King's Theatre then they set off for the Tonypandy Hippodrome in the Rhondda Valley of Wales where the general manager and ringmaster just happened to be their father once again. The following week saw them move a few miles down the road to Porth Hippodrome where no doubt three attractive young ladies would be popular with the mining community families.

By February they were back north in Dewsbury at the Hippodrome where they were 'well received' according to *The Stage* of 2 February 1905.

It would be tedious to record the various theatres they performed in during this year but when the end of the year approached, a new situation arose. An advert in *The Era* for 2 December 1905 was headed:

PAREZ-BANZAI. Six in number
Great musical comedy troupe.
Tuesday and next – Public Hall, Barnsley.

The report for the Barnsley Public Hall dated 9 December 1905 stated 'the Banzai Parez Troupe gives a fine musical turn'. I noted that the Parez-Banzai had now become the Banzai-Parez which may have indicated some early tensions amongst the performers but subsequent adverts and reports stuck to the latter description so the situation must have been resolved. I was able to find later that the Banzai Group were apparently three Japanese men who may have seen the Dale girls as a useful entrée to the northern music hall circuit. I have no information as to how the troupe co-operated but the reports in the trade press were reasonably positive. They were at Ohmy's Circus in Leigh where 'the musical act by the Banzai Troupe is well received' then after the turn of the year they set off on a concert party tour of smaller halls in less frequented locations.

The Victoria Hall, Weston super Mare; Jubilee Hall, Weymouth; Mechanics Hall, Portland; Drill Hall, Bridport; Amity Hall, Poole and the County Hall, Salisbury were visited by the troupe during January and February giving them a grand tour of south west England. They then moved further east to visit St John's Rooms in Winchester; the Town Hall, Chichester; Corn Exchange, Basingstoke; Town Hall, Staines; followed by the public halls in Chertsey, Horsham, Surbiton and Redhill. It was a non-stop weekly visit to presumably small audiences in all these places which had not the population they have now. I think their last appearance as a combined group during this period took place at the Market Hall, Gravesend in mid-April.

The next week an advert in *The Era* referred only to the 'Parez Trio'; the Banzais had disappeared. A further advert dated 12 May 1905 states:

PAREZ TRIO (Sisters)
Fine Musical Act.
Valuable Instruments
Free Monday for a few weeks.
Thanks to Leon Vint for 16 weeks comfortable
engagement.
Comms: Harry Dale 151 Knutsford Road,
Warrington.

Leon Vint, an impresario, must have arranged the grand tour and
brought the two sets of performers together. They certainly had the
opportunity to see the quieter corners of southern England that
three girls from the north might never have visited in their lifetime.

The summer of 1905 was spent at the seaside. Visits to Swansea,
the Pier Pavilion in Hastings and then Dover followed in June and
July. The Banzai Troupe re-appeared in the autumn and early
winter and a report in *The Era* for 9 December 1905 reveals : 'the
Banzai-Parez Troupe give a fine musical turn'.

Ohmy's Circus in Leigh, Lancashire was graced with the troupe
throughout January 1906 and thereafter they set off on their travels
throughout England once again. They started from Weston super
Mare, then went to Weymouth, Portland, Bridport, Poole,
Salisbury, Winchester, Chichester, Basingstoke, Staines, Chertsey,
Horsham, Surbiton, Redhill, Gravesend, High Wycombe, finishing
in Rugby in May.

The acknowledgement to Leon Vint's 16-week tour followed
when the girls moved to the circus in Blackpool in June 1906, but
there are no reports from then until the end of the year about their
activities.

Leon Vint, real name Edward Preston, was an entrepreneur in
the entertainment business. Organising these concert party style
tours around England was probably quite a chore but once he had
the right group of entertainers on his books, it all seemed to go well.
The fact that he had the Banzai-Parez Troupe on tour two years on
the trot reflected both on their professionalism and on their
popularity with the audiences. Vint is known to have bought the St
James Theatre in Long Eaton about 1907 (later renamed the
Coliseum, then the Scala), and was also the proprietor of the
Empire Music Hall in Nuneaton around 1912. Other establishments bearing his name were to be found at Ilkeston,

Loughborough and Neath, for example. He adapted to the changing trends of entertainment, as about the mid-1910s he renamed some of his music halls 'Picturedoms'.

In most of 1907 there are no reports about the Parez Sisters in the trade press, only three or four adverts placed by themselves stating they were 'on tour', but, frustratingly, not saying where. In 1908 information about them emerges once again when an advert in *The Era* dated 28 March 1908 appears:

> PAREZ GIRLS (Trio)
> Handbell Ringers, Xylophonists, Vocalists, Banjoists
> Ninth Year, now vacancies: 167 Knutsford Road,
> Warrington.

I am not clear if the bagpipes had been abandoned at this point, but enlarging their instrumental talents by mastering the xylophone and the banjo as well as their other instruments perhaps gave them more popular appeal. The next week they were in the Queen's Theatre in Dublin which was followed in April with visits to the Empire in Londonderry then the Alhambra in Belfast. Concluding their Irish tour they probably sailed by steamer from Belfast to Glasgow as they performed in the Gaiety Theatre of that city. A week later, in May, they were at the King's Theatre in Kilmarnock then later that month in Macclesfield, at the Theatre Royal. They then moved to Seacombe and the Irving Theatre in June while in October they returned to the Gaiety Theatre in Glasgow followed by an appearance at the New Gaiety, Clydebank, a theatre owned by the impresario, A.E. Pickard, probably best known as proprietor of the Britannia-Panopticon in Glasgow's Trongate. After this came a move to Airdrie Hippodrome. December 1908 was spent in Meltham, Yorkshire, Hadfield, Derbyshire and the Rotherham Hippodrome.

It turned out that 1909 was a significant year for the Dale family with Stanley Henry Dale, the fourth son, starting the ball rolling in January when he married Mary Harper in Latchford, Warrington. Other marriages were to follow.

In the early part of that year the appeal of the Parez Sisters was probably on the wane as they were not being booked into the larger theatres in more significant locations. They were working in smaller towns and in less attractive premises: Langton, Staffs, Oakengates,

Ella Coyne née Dale, with husband Gus Coyne, RFA, and their son. 1916
(Dale Collection)

Salop, the Victoria Hall, Dewsbury, the Parr Hall, Warrington, then the Hippodrome in Stalybridge in early April.

Now the next marriage took place. On 20 April 1909 in Warrington Register Office, Ella Dale, aged 30, married Gustavus Patrick Coyne, of the same age, who was an actor. Gus Coyne was the son of an established Edwardian actor, Gardiner Coyne, who had his own group of players who toured the theatres. The marriage was announced in *The Era* in what can only be described as a show business manner: 'April 20th in Warrington, Gus Coyne-Gardiner (Bronson) son of the late Gardiner Coyne to Miss Ella Parez.' Using stage names seemed to be the normal thing in the trade papers when making birth, marriage and death announcements. This may have been acceptable to the show business readers at that time but for later searchers of family history, it can be misleading, if not deceiving.

I noted that none of Ella's sisters were witnesses to the marriage. The two remaining members of the Parez Trio arranged a double wedding, however, on 8 May 1909 in Lanchester Register Office, Co. Durham. Lottie Dale, aged 25, married John Hindmarsh Howarth, an electrician working in the theatres, and Vera Maud Dale, aged 20, married Walter Lawson, another electrician staying at the same address in Stanley as John Howarth. In the space of three short weeks, three of the daughters of Harry Dale were married and the Parez Trio ceased to exist. No further reference to them as entertainers has been found after this date.

The three sisters had some nine years performing on the music-hall stage, or in the circus arena. They never reached the top rank of entertainment, but seemed to be popular and my impression is that they made a reasonable living. The nature of their act needed constant rehearsal and innovation and I have tried to bring that out in this text. Again, the influence of their father percolates their career. It is almost inevitable that they all married men with connections to the theatre business. The opportunities to meet men from other backgrounds was undoubtedly limited with their six days a week in front of the public, coupled with constant travel the length and breadth of the British Isles. I have no doubt there were publicity photos of the three girls together, but I have never seen any, only individual portraits of Ella, Lottie and Vera Maud have survived.

For interest, I have followed their lives thereafter, and the results have been quite enlightening in several ways.

Ella and Gus Coyne were hardest to trace. As far as I know, Gus Coyne, the actor, was born in 1881 in Dewsbury, Yorkshire and became a 'theatre agent' as recorded in Ella's death certificate. His 'stage name' was Gus Bronson and he appears in the trade press from time to time labelled as an 'advance manager'. With the First World War, he volunteered to join the Royal Field Artillery in December 1915 as part of the 'Pals' battalions and was noted in *The Stage* of 12 August 1916 as a bombardier in the 120th Brigade, RFA. By 16 March according to *The Stage* again, he was now a full corporal. His brother-in-law, Stanley Henry Dale had joined the RFA in November 1915. Sadly, Corporal G.P. Coyne of the 38th Heavy Trench Mortar Battery was killed in action on 15 March 1917 and is buried in Bard Cottage Cemetery near Ypres, in Belgium. I know Ella and he lived in Scarborough for a period after they married, and a couple of postcard photographs confirm that. However, I have not traced any children born to them before Gus was killed, and Ella never remarried. She died aged 87 in February 1965 in Scarborough. A son was the informant and a photo exists of Ella holding a small boy but there is no documentary evidence that he was born to Ella and Gus. He might be an adopted child, but again, I cannot confirm this.

The story of Lottie Dale is equally poignant. After her marriage to John Howarth, she had several children, the first three, all born in Coventry were named Vera Elizabeth (1910), John Hamer (1913), and Dorothy Ella (1915). After the end of the First World War, when her husband had been in the Royal Flying Corps, then the newly formed Royal Air Force, she had a further three all born in Stockton Heath, near Warrington. In 1918 there was Mercia, Lottie was born in 1920 and Frank in 1923. The repetition of Dale family names is quite noticeable. Tragically, Lottie died aged 40 on 23 April 1924, only a few months after her last childbirth but it seems she had been suffering from a debilitating illness for some time before that.

I am indebted to her grandson in Leeds, Kevin Howarth, who traced her family tree and gave me the following information backed up with official documentation. John Hindmarsh Howarth was now a widower with six small children to feed, clothe and care for. It seems he had been having some help in caring for the children and managing the home from a niece through marriage, May Bailey, daughter of Richard and Amy Bailey (née Dale). May must have continued to assist him after his wife died, and the relationship flourished as John Howarth and May Bailey were married on 22 March 1925 in the Independent Methodist Church, Stockton Heath. She was 25 and he was 38 years old. Although a niece, there was no blood relationship between them. As far as is known, there were no children resulting from this marriage. However, May had a sister, two years younger, named Amy, who also seems to have been involved in helping with the family. Amy Bailey gave birth to a daughter in 1930 named Barbara, but the father is not named on the birth certificate. There is conjecture as to who the father might have been.

Vera Maud Lawson, or 'Dot', as she was known in the family, had a marriage that was entwined with sadness. She had a son, Christopher Sydney Lawson in 1911, born in the district of Morpeth, then a second son, Walter, in 1913 who died shortly after birth. A daughter named Dorothy was born in 1921, but the Lawsons lost Christopher in 1928 at only 17 years old. The family lived in Ashington, a large mining village in Northumberland, and it was at Vera's house that her father, Harry Dale, died suddenly in April 1914. In the meantime, Walter Lawson senior became a successful cinema operator in north east England. I have a poor photo of my father looking slightly uncomfortable, with his arm round Dorothy, taken about 1934 when Dad would be aged 26 and Dorothy about 12/13. They were, after all, first cousins. Dorothy married in 1942 to Eric Wilgoose and had a son named Christopher Dale Wilgoose. Vera Maud Lawson died in the summer of 1937 aged 48 in the same geographic area she had lived all her married life. Walter Lawson died in 1956 aged 66 and left all his fortune to his grandson. There is a press cutting from the *Daily Mail* dated 1956 where the young grandson, Dale, aged eight, is asked what he wants in the future, and his response is that he wants to be a chemist.

The last of the five daughters of Harry and Sarah Ann Dale was Doris May Dale born in Warrington on 26 July 1893 at 10 Orford Avenue. I have no evidence she chose to go down the entertainment route like her sisters. The 1901 census showed her as a scholar living at 32 Mill Lane in Warrington, while the 1911 census, when she was 17, taken at 16 Ash Grove, Warrington, describes her as an 'Assistant Tea Sales' so presumably she was employed in a grocer's shop. By this time, the music halls and circus were both under pressure from the cinema – entertainment for the masses. The price of entry to the cinema was cheap, there was a huge and growing variety of films being produced and the programmes were changed at least weekly, sometimes more often. As pure escapism from the everyday toil of

Doris May Lemon, née Dale, with husband Frank and nephew Jack Dale on right at Skegness, 1934 (Dale Collection)

industry and commerce, the cinema at this time had no equal. The First World War was a social milestone in several ways, and one aspect was the decline in the popularity of the music hall and the circus as places of entertainment. Perhaps she made the right decision but as a member of a talented family, possibly something was lost for ever.

Doris May Dale was married on 31 December 1914 aged 21 to Francis Lemon, aged 23, a bachelor glass maker. The ceremony was in the Holy Trinity Church of Warrington and took place nine months after the death of her father, and only four months after the start of the War. The Lemons had four of a family: Edith born in 1916, Joyce in 1919, Frank in 1926 and Alan in 1928. I am aware that up to 1931 the family remained in Warrington as Doris' mother, Sarah Ann Dale, died in her house at 9 Monks Street in 1931. Doris May proved to be a long lifer herself, as she died in October 1986, aged 93 in Portscatho, Cornwall, where her youngest daughter, Joyce, was domiciled. The elder daughter, Edith, had emigrated to Canada.

The Dale daughters showed a range of musical talents. They worked hard and entertained for several years then cut themselves off from their accustomed life and settled into domesticity. Sadly, three of them died comparatively young; Amy, aged 33 after producing five children, Lottie aged 41 after six children and Vera Maud aged 48 after three children. Was there a weakness somewhere in the genes? Their mother was a slight, small person but managed to have 11 children of whom only one was lost at birth, and was 80 when she passed away. As is often the way, the two daughters that did not die early lived beyond the customary span with Ella reaching 87 and Doris May, *la grande dame,* at 93 years.

THE SONS OF HARRY WAMBA DALE

My grandfather, married to Edinburgh-born Jeannie Lavin in 1899, had five children of whom two died leaving three survivors, all boys. The musical gene of the Dale family passed down the line to this next generation and all three, in different ways, became entertainers of one sort or another. The first two boys, Harry, born in 1901, and Jack, born in 1903, after their early education at Bruntsfield Primary School in Edinburgh, left school aged 14 and initially moved into non-musical apprenticeships.

Harry was articled to an engraving company in Edinburgh called T.R. Dale & Co., which as far as I can ascertain, was not related in any way to our family. He started his apprenticeship there but the start of the First World War in August 1914 interrupted his training. His army papers, which have survived, confirm he was in training as an apprentice when he volunteered as a boy, for the 3/9th Royal Scots. A letter dated October 1915 in the Army papers addressed to the 'officer commanding 3/9 (Highlanders) Royal Scots' states: 'I am quite willing that my son Harry Dale shall join the 3/9 (Highlanders) as a bugler. L/Cpl H.W. Dale.' His father probably arranged this situation so that his eldest son could be with him in the same battalion, which was not a 'service' battalion, but one concerned with training. Perhaps Harry Wamba Dale was prescient, seeing the war dragging on and that as his son approached the age of 18, there was a strong likelihood he would have become a front line soldier.

In fact, son Harry, after joining, learnt to play the trombone in the military band, and there is a photo of the band taken at a camp near Hawick, in the Scottish Borders, with him standing behind his father, the band corporal, with a trombone in his hand (see p.136).

I have also drawn attention to the arrival in the same band of Harry Wamba Dale's younger brother, Sydney, who was already a professional trombonist. I am certain Uncle Sydney gave young

3/9th Royal Scots military band; Corporal Harry Dale with cornet in front row, his eldest son Harry, fourth from left back row, 1916 (Dale Collection)

Harry many technical and musical tips to assist him. He was too young to face any enemy bullets so when the First World War ended, young Harry was demobbed and assigned to the Territorials, the 4th Battalion, as he was now 18 years old. He returned to Edinburgh and his apprenticeship, also getting involved in the Scout Movement at Christ Church, Morningside, a Scottish Episcopalian Church in the south side of the city. As part of his apprenticeship training he attended the Art College in Edinburgh and was, by this time, also playing the trombone semi-professionally around the dance halls and in musical events in the Scottish capital. There is a photograph extant of a 14 piece mid-1920s dance band led by Reynolds Payne in Edinburgh with Harry Dale one of two trombonists in the front row.

Another popular nine-piece dance band in Edinburgh during the 1920s was J. Sutherland & his London Riviera Dance Orchestra', a rather long name, but whether this band ever performed in London or on the Riviera is not known. A photograph shows the Sutherland twins, James and John on piano and drums respectively, with Harry Dale the sole trombonist, and younger brother Jack Dale one of the saxophone/clarinet players (see opposite).

Moving on towards the end of the 1920s, Jack had become

quite ambitious, and moved south of the border, permanently playing in dance bands in Birmingham and Leicester. He formed his own four-piece dance band and took it to the Café Dansant in Skegness over the summer season in 1929, and was a great success. Returning in 1930, he included older brother Harry in the five-piece line-up and they had a favourable write-up in the *Lincolnshire Chronicle* while *The Era* of 16 July 1930 comments on the versatility of the players at the Café Dansant with 'Harry Dale, trombone, vibraphone and bass' and he was also known to be a 'capital vocalist', such that the band made a 'speciality of vocal choruses'. Jack and Harry returned to Skegness again in 1931 and once more received positive write-ups by the local *Skegness News*. About this time, Harry Dale was invited to join another popular dance band of the time led by Benny Loban.

Loban was born to Jewish parents in Ukraine but his family moved to Canada about 1913 to avoid persecution under the pogroms. He was a talented violinist receiving some training in London at the Royal Academy of Music. He returned to Canada but with little work available at that time he soon came back to London in the 1920's and led small ensembles and dance bands in the capital. His big break came when he led the Savoy Orpheans Dance Orchestra about 1930. This well-known dance band had played at the Savoy Hotel in the Strand during the 1920s and one

J. SUTHERLAND & his LONDON - RIVIERA Dance Orchestra

Harry Dale with trombone on right. Jack Dale with saxophone, third on left. Edinburgh 1924 (Dale Collection)

of the leaders, Ben Evers, had reformed it about 1929. Benny Loban became the conductor and made a couple of records in 1930, where one of the saxophonists was Jack Dale. However, the Savoy Hotel objected to the use of their name so Loban used the title 'Music Weavers' and established a nine-piece band.

The *Melody Maker* of December 1930 comments on the formation of this band which opened at the Bristol Hippodrome on 8 December with Harry Dale on the trombone and Jack Dale as first saxophone. The rest of the line-up was second and third saxophone, drums, trumpet, bass and banjo. The same trade paper noted 'Benny Loban and his Music Weavers' taking the stage at the Ayr Gaiety Theatre in June 1931 and staying for the season until October. Again, Harry Dale was the trombonist but Jack Dale had left by his time and was creating his own music elsewhere. For two or three years Loban had the 'Music Weavers' in Ayr in the summer season, then at the West End Dance Hall in Birmingham for the winter season. His band performed on BBC Midland radio in 1933 and details can be found in the next chapter on Jack Dale. Benny Loban and his Music Weavers also made records at this time – but I have never been able to find any from this period – and it is pretty certain the trombonist was still Harry Dale. Trade papers in 1934 list the band members and Harry Dale was the trombonist, with a number of other players repeated each year, showing loyalty to

Bandleader Benny Loban in centre with the Music Weavers, 1931; Harry Dale far left (Dale Collection)

Loban, but also how popular the band was in the dance halls of Scotland and England.

Benny Loban continued his dance-band leadership throughout the later 1930s but without the Dale brothers to assist him. He played at the popular Palais Ballroom in Glasgow throughout the Second World War and broadcast on VE Day. With the decline of Big Band Music after the war, he returned to Canada about 1952 and was successful in real estate, dying in Toronto in 1993.

In a previous chapter I have shown that Harry Wamba Dale deserted his wife and family after 1918. His son, Harry Dale, filled the vacuum and became the parent substitute of his two younger brothers, Jack and Bert. Harry stayed as a boarder in Bryson Road in Edinburgh with a family named Hardie, while Jack was also a boarder for a spell before going south to England to develop his musical career. Because of all this disruption, my dad, Bert, lived with his grandparents, Maggie and Patrick Lavin in McNeill Street, Edinburgh, but more of this later.

Harry, aged 32, married Helen Hardie, known as 'Ella', the daughter of his landlord, in June 1933 in Edinburgh. The best man was my dad looking slightly self conscious in a smart suit with white gloves in hand. Harry kept up his professional playing with Benny Loban but after 1934 I think he returned to Edinburgh and took up his trade as a skilled engraver. He worked with a company named Gilbert E. Oliver located in St James Square, just behind Register House at the east end of Princes Street, long since demolished. He was known to have a particularly high ability as an engraver long before machine engraving arrived on the scene. Most of his work was commercial in nature – letterheads, business cards and so on. He was asked to make a plate for a new issue of a Scottish banknote. Each colour in the banknote required a separate plate and to prevent forgeries, each plate went to a different engraver. It was vital all the plates came together in the final printing process. To be asked to make such a contribution was quite an accolade.

Harry and Ella had a son in May 1934 named Alan. He is my only Dale first cousin and we are in touch regularly although he resides in England and I live in Edinburgh. Alan gave me details of his dad's life that have filled many of the gaps in my knowledge of the family. Harry worked primarily as an engraver during the day and played professionally in the evening in and around Edinburgh.

When the Second World War started in 1939, he was 38 years old and whilst not immediately called up, he joined the local volunteer fire service. As the war progressed he was finally summoned for King and Country, joining the RAF in March 1944 as a radar operator, at that time a new technology, in the Shetland Islands. His musical talents were quickly recognised so he spent a lot of his spare time maintaining the morale of the locals by playing throughout the islands at social events such as ceilidhs. Demobbed in early 1946, he returned to Edinburgh where, tragically, his wife Ella died in June 1946 from asthmatic complications.

He continued to play the trombone with a well-known local bandleader – Tim Wright. Tim Wright had several bands of different combinations and sizes, especially those performing Scottish dance music, but Harry's preference was the smaller ensemble where his skill would be more useful and musical variety was required. My cousin told me that this small band played at the Cavendish Ballroom, Tollcross, in Edinburgh, – an establishment that still exists but in a much altered form – and was so popular that Tim Wright suggested they tone down their final session because the big band due on next was getting restless at the standing ovations from the patrons! Praise indeed!

Harry Dale married again in July 1948 to Beatrice Anderson, who was the office manager at the engraving company where he worked, and my dad was again the best man. Harry reduced his playing as he got older – he was now suffering from bronchitis brought on by smoking. He was an excellent and enthusiastic gardener and enjoyed golf and bowls. My dad and he were particularly close due to the problems of their childhood. My dad once told me that without Harry to guide and protect him when he was young, he may have left the straight path he was on and become a quite different person. Harry Dale passed away aged 73 from a heart problem in April 1974.

I have devoted a complete chapter to the next brother in line – Jack Dale – as he achieved some fame over many years as a dance band leader, so I will complete this chapter with some information about my father.

Albert Stanley Ernest Dale was born on 30 April 1908, the last child of Harry Wamba and Jeannie Lavin Dale. The house where he was born still exists in Viewforth Square, Edinburgh. The first few years of his life were a bit chaotic. His father was away a lot of the time leading circus orchestras in various parts of the country throwing a lot of responsibility on Jeannie to raise three boisterous boys. The war commenced in August 1914, and my grandfather volunteered for the Army a year later in 1915 when dad was about seven. Once more Dad was on his own and with the reduction in income, the family had to move to a small basement house in the Tollcross area of the city. I think there had been tensions between Jeannie and Harry before the war started, but after his departure to serve the King, she took to the bottle. It is a sadly familiar problem and my dad was in the middle of it. Harry junior was also in the Army and Jack was living with his grandmother, as there was no room in the basement house for the two brothers together.

My dad said in his memoirs that he thought his mother was just lonely, as she had parties in the house with a variety of strange friends and acquaintances appearing each time. For a young, impressionable child, it was not the right environment, and one night everything came to a head. A party was in full swing just before Christmas 1916 when his mother either cut herself with a knife or someone else cut her, it is not clear. There was blood every-where and Dad started to scream. He got a wallop on the head for his pains from his mother then ran screaming up the stairs to the

Harry, Bert and Jack Dale, the sons of Harry Wamba Dale, in 1952, Edinburgh (Dale Collection)

street and ran to Jeannie's sister, Nellie, who lived nearby. He banged on her door until she let him in and calmed him down. He stayed the night with her then she sent for the authorities. What happened to Jeannie and her so-called friends is not known, but Dad was transferred to an establishment called 'The Children's Shelter' in the centre of Edinburgh, and taken into care.

He was there for a few weeks over Christmas, but as far as he was concerned, it was good, as he had plenty to eat and lots of toys to play with. The children had a Christmas Party which he enjoyed as he imitated Charlie Chaplin and everyone laughed. Then he realised he had a hole in his trousers and his shirt was hanging out. His father, Harry Wamba Dale, was sent for who took him out of the shelter and arranged for Dad's mother's parents, Patrick and Maggie Lavin, to look after him at their house in McNeill Street. His mother never came to see him but surprised everyone by suddenly joining the Women's Army Auxiliary Corps, which had been established in 1917. She was stationed near Perth until the end of the war. Dad settled in at McNeill Street and soon had plenty young friends of his own age.

At the end of the war, Jeannie Dale returned to Edinburgh and rented a small flat for herself, living alone. Harry Wamba Dale had also returned in late 1916, staying with his brother Albert in Lothian Street. He and Albert were playing in the orchestra of the Theatre Royal, and every Wednesday evening Dad and brother Jack went to the Theatre Royal using tickets from their father. Dad now regarded his grandparents as his parents. Patrick Lavin was diabetic and ill most of the time, so was not an active grandfather. Granny Maggie Lavin was strict but fair, and had certain rules. One was that young Albert could have a slice of bread with either margarine or jam, but not both at the same time. Dad pondered this for a while, then one evening he took the slice of bread, cut it in half, and put margarine on one half and jam on the other. Granny Lavin promptly clipped his ear for being smart! I think it was an inspired initiative!

Dad went to Boroughmuir Secondary School, which he enjoyed, leaving at 14 years old. He worked briefly for Edinburgh Parish Council as an office boy before finding a job with a manufacturing stationers; Andersons Edinburgh Ltd. His father had gone in 1918 to look for musical work in London and the south, eventually settling in Hartlepool in north-east England. There was little or no regular contact between the three brothers and their father. I have tried to show in previous chapters how the Dale family instructed their children in music and the entertainment business, but in my dad's case, the line stopped rather suddenly. Although Jeannie Dale remained in Edinburgh, she led her own life and again there was minimal contact between her and her sons.

My father's interest as a young man was primarily in sport and the Boys' Brigade. He was a good footballer playing in one of the leading amateur sides, named Northern Amateurs and winning an impressive collection of medals which I still have. He also played cricket in the summer and had some athletic abilities as well. He did inherit a fine baritone voice and although he could not read music, his singing, the few times I heard him, was of a good standard. Later, he bought a ukelele and taught himself to play, imitating the very popular north of England music-hall and film star, George Formby, and his nonsense songs.

In 1937, at the age of 29 he was promoted to warehouse manager in Edinburgh with Anderson's, and in that year he married my mum, Cissie Nelson in July. He lost his mother Jeannie in November the same year, as she succumbed at 60 to cancer. I arrived in early 1939, then the Second World War started in September of the same year. My mother did not have any more children.

Dad volunteered for the Royal Air Force in 1940, romantically wanting to be a pilot, but aged 32 he was regarded at that stage of the war as being too old, so was allocated a ground crew position instead. With hindsight, I am grateful for this RAF decision as the death rate amongst aircrew, especially in Bomber Command, was horrendous. His sporting and fitness abilities were quickly recognised and in 1942 he was commissioned as an 'acting pilot officer unpaid' moving into the Physical Fitness branch, responsible for survival training and the fitness of bomber crews. It was at this stage that his Dale entertaining genes started to emerge. Station concert parties were an essential feature for maintaining the morale of the bomber crews, and Dad threw himself into this with his customary enthusiasm. He was based principally at three RAF stations: Middleton St George in Teesside, where the bomber crews were mainly Canadian; Market Harborough; and Moreton in Marsh.

Whilst in the Cotswolds with my wife a few years ago, we stayed in Moreton in Marsh, and on leaving our hotel in the morning, my attention was caught by a notice directing anyone interested to the Wellington Aviation Museum, where the history of Moreton in Marsh bomber station was explained. I was emotionally affected when I casually mentioned to the curator, Gerry Tyzack, that my dad had been the PFO (Physical Fitness Officer) at Moreton in 1944 and 1945. Without hesitation, Gerry went to a shelf and produced programmes of the station concert party entitled 'To See Such Fun' and photographs of dad – Flight Lieutenant Dale – performing on stage in front of a live audience as a singer, actor and comedian. This particular concert party was

Bert Dale right with Dick Richards, entertaining RAF personnel at Moreton in Marsh, 1945 (Dale Collection)

so popular it was asked by the Air Ministry to make a tour of other RAF stations in the London area and was apparently well received everywhere it went. I cherish the photographs as they showed my Dad doing what three generations of the Dale family had been doing for years – entertaining a live audience.

He was demobbed at the end of January 1946 and returned to civilian life, working as a commercial traveller for a Glasgow greetings card and calendar printing company, Millar & Lang Ltd. He never developed his entertaining skills beyond the odd song and a good story telling ability preferring to maintain his interest in sport. After his football days were over, he developed a passion for golf, table tennis and bowling, reaching a high standard in all three. He was, if nothing else, a competitive person. He had always shown a lot of discipline, being a total abstainer from alcohol, based I suspect on the problems he witnessed and endured as a small child. He never smoked, regarding it as unhealthy, so it was quite a shock when he turned 70 and found himself with chest pains on the golf course. A heart problem was diagnosed and a by-pass operation was suggested.

He and I spoke about this as the doctors said he could carry on as he was and would probably have another couple of years but perhaps he would need a wheel chair in due course. The operation, a major one in 1979 when the technology was not as advanced as it is now, could ease his problem and give him several years of reasonable living but there was a risk at his age. He bravely chose the operation as, having been active all his life, he could not face a time when he would be chair or bed ridden. Although the operation was a success, there were complications immediately after, and he died a few days later in the hospital, a week before his 71st birthday.

He was a great loss to me and to my three children whom he adored. He did leave a lot of information about himself in the form of press cuttings, letters, photographs and other memorabilia. Perhaps he did not follow in the footsteps of other members of the Dale family but he certainly entertained – on the football pitch, the golf course, the cricket square and the bowling green. He also entertained his three grandchildren and if circumstances were appropriate, he could sing a song, strum the ukelele, and tell a good story with a well-timed punch line. The genes were there, perhaps a bit subdued, but available when required!

JACK LAVIN DALE
AND THE DANCING YEARS

y dad's older brother was John Lavin Dale, born on 23
January 1903 at 36 Grassmarket, Edinburgh. The
Grassmarket has become quite a trendy location in
Edinburgh these 21st-century days, but in Edwardian times it was a
part of the city where there was a high percentage of poor families
living in high density housing, many of whom were Irish
immigrants. It was a broad street with three- and four-storey
tenements, inns, stables, lodging houses and the old Cornmarket,
and was always busy. Jack's middle name, Lavin, is Irish, and was,
of course, the maiden name of his mother, Jeannie Ferguson Lavin.
Jack, as he was always known, wrote a brief resumé of his life
prompted by the death of my father in 1979, giving me some useful
information about our specific branch of the Dale family. When he
wrote his resumé, he was well into his seventies and I was impressed
at the amount of detail he remembered, going back into his early
childhood. When researching family history, one of the essential
requirements is to ask older members of the family to put their
recollections on paper, or, alternatively, interview them in a gentle
and participative manner. The amount of information garnered in
this way can be very helpful, and even if there are errors in some
facts, such as dates, names, locations, and so on, these can often be
corrected when the researcher has access to official documentation,
or other members of the same family are asked to comment.

Some of Jack's earliest memories as a child concerned his father
when he was performing in the theatre orchestra at the King's
Theatre, Leven Place, in Edinburgh. One famous international
performer who stayed in the Dale household, which was close to
the King's, was the Polish pianist, Jan Paderewski. He visited
Edinburgh in the autumn of 1912 and Jack, aged nine, recalled his
'fluffy white hair, moustache, and piercing eyes'. Paderewski was
active in the cause of Polish independence and became the Republic
of Poland's first prime minister in 1919; he died in 1941.

When the First World War commenced, as explained in a previous chapter, Jack's father, Harry Wamba Dale, volunteered for the Royal Scots. When Jack was 14, he also joined up (in August 1917) as a boy bugler but his father at this time had left the Army due to his age. Jack was only 4'6" when he joined, and a special uniform had to be made for him including a Hunting Stewart tartan kilt of the 9th Battalion, Royal Scots. I possess an amusing studio photograph of him in his uniform looking proudly at the camera, while on the back it is addressed to his Aunty Nellie, his mother's sister. As a band boy, based in Edinburgh Castle, he had a variety of tasks, including making tea for the rest of the band. When cleaning up one day, he picked up a mug with water in it and emptied it out of the window of the barracks which were located high above the castle rock facing the south of the city. Unfortunately, the mug held the teeth of bandsman Lance Corporal McDonald, so all the band boys were sent down to the rocks below the window to look for the vital teeth. They were found undamaged after an intensive search and all was calm once again!

The military band participated in church parades on Sundays, marching from the Castle perhaps half a mile down the High Street to St Giles' Cathedral. For his first parade, Jack was allocated the cymbals but after 100 yards he could not hold the heavy brass cymbals up any more, so after the parade, the bandmaster, Sergeant Dan Sweeney, decided he should learn the clarinet and also be a regimental bugler and drummer. Jack fell in love with the clarinet, and later the saxophone, and his army musical training stood him in good stead for his later life. From the Castle, he was transferred to Maryhill Barracks in Glasgow for a spell, then Cupar in Fife, and was eventually demobbed from there in 1919. His Army duties had been mainly ceremonial and I am not even sure he fired a rifle.

A couple of photos exist showing Jack as a drummer with the 9th Royal Scots pipe band, and also as a clarinettist with the military band (see p.100). He was only 16 when he left the Army, but his two years in uniform were character forming and taught him to stand up for himself.

He then took up an engineering apprenticeship with Brown Brothers, an Edinburgh-based marine engineering company, from 1919 to 1926. He told me he was earning 12 shillings a week as an apprentice, but in the evenings he played in a dance band earning

about £4 a week at 'Maximes' in Tollcross, a popular dance hall that
still exists but under a different name. He then moved to the
Sutherland Dance Band with his brother Harry and this was a good
grounding for him. This nine-piece band played in the popular
Palais-de-Danse, Fountainbridge, and also toured in the summer
months.

The Dale brothers played locally and had their first BBC radio
broadcasting experience in 1926 augmenting a small ensemble led
by another local Edinburgh band leader, Herbert More. The
broadcast was made in the Assembly Rooms, George Street, in the
days when the soloists had to face a wall with a piano behind them
because of the acoustics! The technology has moved on a bit since
these early days!

Domestically, he briefly stayed with his mother in a rented flat
in Edinburgh after she returned from her war service, but they did
not get on too well so he decided to head off down south to the
English Midlands seeking fame and fortune. His father had
departed south of the border in about 1918 and he and Jack did not
meet up again until 1930 when Harry Wamba Dale was living and
working in Hartlepool.

Jack Dale and his band, Skegness 1930; Harry Dale second on left, Jack in the
middle (Dale Collection)

After playing with bands in the Birmingham area for a spell, Jack put together a four-piece band and obtained the contract to play at the Café Dansant ('The Ballroom in a Garden') at Skegness in Lincolnshire. An advertising leaflet shows the opening of the season on Saturday 18 May 1929 with 'Music by Jack Dale and his Band, direct from his successful season in Scotland.' The commitment seemed quite onerous with the band playing from 11 a.m. to 12.30 p.m., then performing for tea dances from 4 p.m. to 6 p.m. every day, and evening dances on Fridays and Saturdays from 9 p.m. until midnight. Skegness was a very popular location for seaside holidays at that time, in the late 1920s, early 1930s.

I am not sure about the claim that Jack was 'direct from his successful season in Scotland' but evidence in previous chapters has shown that members of the Dale family were not averse to blowing their own trumpet, or in Jack's case, clarinet/saxophone, if it achieved a positive result. If he took a gamble in Skegness then it paid off as the local *Lincolnshire Chronicle* commented on the 'rhythmical music played by Jack Dale and his band' and that 'the band has been commended for its programme of dance music at the afternoon and evening dances'. The *Skegness News* specifically praised Jack as a 'versatile performer on the alto and soprano saxes, and the clarinet.'

Benny Loban featured in Jack's musical life as mentioned in the chapter on his brother, Harry. Both brothers played together for the 1930 winter season with Loban under the banner of 'The Savoy Orpheans'. In the summer of 1930 Jack was back in Skegness but now with a five-piece band of brother Harry, trombone, vibraphone and bass; Jack Burnell, piano; James Stephens, drums; and Frank Rothwell, violin and guitar. *The Era* of 16 July 1930 comments 'Jack Dale and his band are doing well at the Café Dansant. They feature many instruments between them'.

The winter season of 1932 saw Jack established at the Palais de Danse, Leicester, leading an orchestra called 'The Orpheans'. The Savoy Hotel in London had objected to the 'Savoy' name appearing on dance-hall bill boards, so by dropping the hotel name, Jack still had a band name well recognised by the enthusiastic patrons of the time. To emphasise the connection, the advertisements stated the 'The Orpheans, Under the Direction of Jack Dale (Late of the Savoy Orpheans)'. The band performed from 8 p.m. to midnight on weekdays, and the admission price was 2 shillings and sixpence,

Jack Dale and his dance band, Leicester Palais de Danse, 1934 (Dale Collection)

or 12.5p in decimal coinage. More praise followed in the local press, about the style and tempo of the music.

The Benny Loban band was contracted to play in Birmingham in the winter months of 1933, and an invitation was received from the BBC Midland Region, for radio broadcasts. I have found references in *The Radio Times* during January and February 1933 for 'Benny Loban and his Music Weavers' when they played on 16 and 23 January, then 4, 13 and 25 February. In all cases the programmes were played live from the West End Dance Hall in Birmingham. There is also a grainy photograph published on 13th February showing the Music Weavers with Harry Dale and trombone, and Jack Dale with saxophone. The venue was another interesting coincidence, as Jack's father, Harry Wamba Dale, was musical director of Bostock's Circus and Menagerie in 1911, when they performed in the Curzon Hall, which in later years was refurbished and reopened in 1925 as the West End Dance Hall.

A pattern then evolved with Jack taking a small band to the Café Dansant in the summer season and a larger band to the Leicester Palais de Danse in the winter months. He performed in Skegness from 1929 until 1934, and in Leicester from 1932 until 1937. However, the local council in Skegness decided to change their summer programme and Jack's contract was not renewed after 1934. Armed with good references, recommendations and lots of press cuttings, the summer season of 1935 was spent at Shanklin Pier on the Isle of Wight. A local press comment on his Shanklin appearance states: 'There is such a snap and rhythm in their playing that the temptation to dance is irresistible. There is no doubt that Jack's Band is the most popular that has ever performed on the Pier.'

A major milestone then took place about this time as the BBC radio sought him out and invited him and his band to perform on the Midland Region wavelength. I think his first BBC broadcast was on 4 February 1934 when he filled in for another band, then this was immediately followed by a successful musical play called 'Ten a Penny' which went out on 7 February 1934 from Birmingham, and there was a further recording of the play for use in 'the British colonies' on 1 June. Never one to miss a trick, Jack renamed his band 'The Midland Regional Broadcasting Band' and in his 1936 summer season, spent at the New Palace Pier, St Leonards-on-Sea, Hastings, he used this title on a couple of colourful posters that I found amongst his surviving papers (see p.152).

More positive events took place in the winter of 1934 as he was successful in getting the dance band contract for the Masque Ballroom, Walford Road, Sparkbrook in Birmingham. This ballroom was regarded as intimate in style with Art Deco decor and a medium-sized floor, and all patrons were expected to be smartly dressed. It was owned at that time by members of the Gilbey family, perhaps better known for their wines and spirits business. The charges for an evening's dancing in 1939 were 3 shillings for a single, and 5 shillings for a double. The Masque closed down in 1955 and became a private social club. There is still a community building on the site but the unique façade has changed and the former dance hall is now used for wedding receptions and other functions.

Jack's crowded diary meant playing in Leicester during the autumn for a restricted number of weeks then moving to Birmingham for a six-month engagement at 'The Masque'. His work at the Palais de Danse, Leicester continued until 1937 but he concentrated on the Birmingham contract from 1934 onwards.

I possess a piece of sheet music entitled 'My Past', a waltz ballad written by Wilfred J. Allington with music by Harold P. Evans published in 1934, which has a photograph of Jack Dale and his

1936 poster. Palace Pier, St Leonards (Hastings) (Dale Collection)

band on the front alongside the caption 'Featured with Enormous Success by Jack Dale'. He may have been promoted on other sheet music – a highly competitive business in the 1930s – but that is the only one I have in my possession. I understand Jack also made a few dance band records of the old 78 rpm type, but, I am not aware of any that have survived into the 21st century.

The BBC broadcast of the musical play in February 1934 did open the door for Jack and his band but the BBC producer did not acknowledge their performance until over a year later. A letter from the producer, Martyn Webster, dated 27 February 1935, did apologise for the delay but assured Jack he was 'trying my best to get you a broadcast from our studios'. A follow-up letter dated 21 March expressed disappointment that Jack was not too keen to broadcast an 'Old Time Programme' but then held out the bait by saying that 'we only allow bands which we think are in the first rank to put over this type of show, and if you make a success of this … I shall do all I can to get you another broadcast doing modern numbers.' Jack wisely, if reluctantly, performed the Old Time dance music programme, but later broadcasts showed he was adding on more modern tunes and a press report in 1935 states: 'The numbers will be presented so as to cover the various periods of dance music.' He had a 40-minute slot on the Midland Region and I noted by 1937 the *Radio Times* was headlining the programme as 'Dancing Time, with Jack Dale and his band'.

The summer season of 1937 was spent at the Plaza Ballroom, Jersey, Channel Islands. This ballroom was unusual in possessing a 'cool and restful sliding roof' and local reports stated

> 'the holiday spirit was rife … the carnival dance attracted 400 people dancing to the music of Jack Dale and Miss Iris Barnes, the champion tap dancer of England, also entertained. The band wore white shirts and black bow ties which allowed them to play the hottest numbers without feeling too hot.'

This particular band was a seven-piece outfit with all the musicians able to perform on more than one instrument. One highly versatile member, besides Jack himself, was Steve Chalmers on clarinet, saxophone and piano, who was also a fine vocalist and clever arranger.

The year 1937 saw an interesting interview with Martyn
Webster, the Midland Region BBC producer, in the *Radio Pictorial*
of 9 July who was commenting on bands playing in the Midlands:
'A band that impressed me by its versatility was that of Jack Dale.'
There then followed a brief biography of Jack which, knowing his
background as I do, could be described in Churchillian terms, as
straying from the narrow path of veracity. His father, apparently,
was a 'Professor of Music, who had little opinion of Jack's early
talent'. In his early days Jack was playing at a music hall where the
public played a new game of pitching coins into his saxophone. 'I
found that very lucrative – eleven and fourpence to be exact, he
recalls with a smile.' It all made good copy, however, and in a more
serious tone, Jack 'considered himself fortunate in finding the right
kind of fellows for his bands and he rarely has trouble with his
musicians, though he makes big demands on their versatility'.

Amongst the letters I found after he died were a number from
sheet music publishers, mainly based in London, thanking him for
playing their music on his radio broadcast programmes. I suspect
the BBC would not have approved of him 'plugging' these tunes
but the Corporation would have been hard pushed to prove
anything untoward. What Jack got out of doing this is not known.

Two examples: first, a letter dated 5 January 1937 headed the
'Cinephone Music Company Ltd, 2–4 Dean Street, London' which
states:

> Dear Jack,
> Just a line to say how much I enjoyed your broadcast last
> night and to thank you for including the two numbers 'Sky
> High Honeymoon' and 'The Fleet's in Port Again' as
> promised.
> Yours sincerely,
> Jim Bailey,
> Professional Department.

Then secondly from the 'Irwin Dash Music Co Ltd, 10 Denmark
Street, London' dated 8 February 1937 Stan Bradbury writes:

> Dear Jack,
> I heard your broadcast on Thursday … thanks ever so
> much for doing 'I Dream of San Marino', it is a pity you

having to cut out 'In the Chapel in the Moonlight' but I hope on the next occasion you will be able to fix me a couple of tunes in. Here's very much appreciating what you have done.

I also found in his papers a contract from the BBC dated March 1939 for a broadcast on 27 April from Birmingham from 9.30 p.m. to 10 p.m. where the band 'of ten players and personal appearance of Jack Dale' were to be paid £18.10 shillings (£18.50). On the back was a list of the music he was going to play consisting of his signature tune 'Goodbye Blues', then a further 12 tunes including evergreens such as 'Jeepers Creepers', 'Penny Serenade' and 'Mexicale Rose'. At the foot of the page in capital red letters was the warning 'Song plugging and the acceptance of free orchestrations are barred and will be considered a breach of contract.'

Life was probably quite comfortable for him in the days before the Second World War. He was living in Birmingham but travelling throughout the country with his bands, reinforced with his broad-casting contracts. When the war started in September 1939 the dance band music scene changed virtually overnight. Birmingham and its environs was a major industrial centre and a prime target for German bombers and the dance halls were too susceptible due to the number of people assembled in one place. Jack patriotically volunteered for the RAF aged 37 and I have a photograph of him at Morecambe in 1940 where he did his 'square bashing'. I found it fascinating that in the First World War he and his brother Harry were both in the Army, but next time he and his two brothers, Harry and Bert, all ended up in the RAF. No wonder Hitler threw in the towel!

Jack's days in the RAF were restricted to about 12 months as the munitions industry, vigorously managed by Lord Beaverbrook, needed trained engineers and his paper qualifications showed he had served his time as an engineer. As a result he was allocated to Midland munitions factories first in Coventry, then in Leicester, where the principal products were anti-aircraft shells. Later, he did manage to smuggle a small example out of the factory where it was destined to be made into a cigarette lighter, but that never happened and the empty one pound shell is still retained in the family.

The day job was important but he was soon on the road again

with a series of dance bands. The government recognised that morale was vital amongst a population being subjected to nightly bombing raids and daily reports in the press of disasters throughout the Empire as Germany, Italy and Japan turned the screw. Dancing was very popular during the war. It was a form of escapism as well as a means of meeting partners of the opposite sex and when the Americans arrived later in the war, they brought their own vigorous styles of dance and music with them that added to the variety of entertainment available.

Jack was back in the Masque Ballroom, Sparkbrook, Birmingham in the winter of 1940, travelling from the munitions factory to play in the evening, and the records show his was to become the residential band there up to 1948. During the summer months of 1941 he took his band further afield with, for example, a June concert in the Plaza Cinema, Gloucester, (see opposite) featuring well known radio stars of the time including Geoffrey Kay, a 17-year-old accordionist. In July Jack was at the Odeon Cinema in Shirley, near Solihull, where the stars included Stanelli and Dick Lawler, Lilian Mann and Walter Bennett, while the New Theatre Royal in Wolverhampton saw Jack Dale and his Midland Broadcasting Band 'play a well balanced selection of light music and jazz and caused a riot of laughter as the bandsmen took part in a funny game of charades'.

The Masque Ballroom in the winter months became a centre for serious amateur competition dancing. The manager, Mr J.H. Harrison, produced a detailed leaflet for 1943 advertising the 'Masque Open Amateur Challenge Cup' with heats for the waltz, foxtrot, tango and quickstep on successive Friday evenings, and 'the Grand Final on 26th March'. The cup was solid silver with miniatures to be retained by the winners. The leaflet comments:

> No competition can be a success without an efficient band. In our Musical Director, Mr Jack Dale, we have one of the most versatile leaders in the country. With his great experience of competitions, we have no doubt that the orchestra, under his direction, will satisfy all.

Jack's hard work did not go unnoticed as he received a benefit from the Masque directors. A letter he kept from George Shelvoke, a director of the Masque, dated 4 February 1943, said 'the directors of

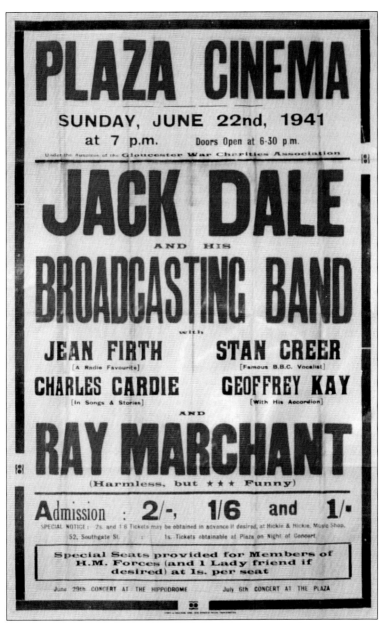

1941 poster advertising Jack Dale's band in Gloucester (Dale Collection)

the Masque appreciate the efforts you have made, often in difficult circumstances, to maintain a high and adequate standard of playing … it was to mark their appreciation and as a gesture of goodwill to yourself that this Benefit was arranged.'

The Dancing Times of November 1944 carried an article by Alex Moore in which he writes:

> 'I doubt whether any provincial hall has done more to encourage good dancing … than the Masque Ballroom at Birmingham. Practically every professional demonstration couple in the country has been booked with Thursday night as 'Dancers Night'. I confess the atmosphere is most refreshing after the blare and blast encountered in many London halls … and a Distinguished Conduct Medal should go to Jack Denny and Jack Dale of the Masque …'

Jack's munitions work ceased in 1945, but the amateur dance competition, started in the war years, continued after the war ended allowing Jack and his band a steady income alongside his many radio broadcasts. He estimated he performed over 200 times in front of a BBC microphone stopping around 1950.

On 15 May 1948 his contract with the Masque Ballroom was not renewed, and the Birmingham *Evening Despatch* ran a feature praising him for developing a 'Birmingham Style' of dance music where rhythm and tempo, coupled with quality orchestrations, were his secrets of success. As a result of the contract termination, he published a promotional leaflet giving many quotes about his band and himself, and sought engagements for bands of any size within the Midlands, or beyond.

A big event for him in 1948 was playing at the 47th Annual Conference of the Labour Party in Scarborough from 17 to 21 May. The Labour government had swept to power at the end of the war and playing on such an occasion was a major accolade for him. However, I am afraid his politics, at least when I got to know him later when he was a good bit older, were definitely not of a socialist inclination. Slightly to the right of Genghis Khan might be a closer definition!

The band played three times according to the conference programme: on Tuesday 18 May at a civic reception in the Spa Ballroom, repeated on 19 May at a second reception, then finally on

20 May at a reception in the same ballroom, organised by the Scarborough & Whitby Divisional Labour Party. All the major Labour government ministers were present at the conference so I like to think he entertained them well, and perhaps had an opportunity to speak to a few of them.

In the summer of 1948 he was playing at the Tower Ballroom, Edgbaston described as 'Birmingham's largest and most beautiful ballroom by the lake'. The adverts show that he was responding to the changing demands of the patrons with 'Old Tyme Dancing' on Wednesday nights, 'Jive' on Monday and ordinary dance nights on the Friday and Saturday.

His success and popularity at the Labour Party Conference paid off as he was back at the Scarborough Spa Ballroom again in the summer of 1949 for the season and the *Scarborough Evening News* of 10 September carried a photo of him (see p.161). The council entertainment's guide also shows that Jack gave light music concerts every afternoon as well as dance music programmes each evening. He and his colleagues worked long hours over the season but I recollect his comment that he enjoyed every minute.

By this time, however, the music business was changing and the big dance orchestras were not as popular as they had been. Dance styles were changing, popular music was in transition, and the influence from across the Atlantic through films, records and visiting performers was significant. He kept up his advertising campaign offering bands of different sizes tailored to suit special occasions but it was hard work. In 1950 he was 47 years old and had been on the road since about 1924.

His life had also changed domestically as he had married in 1946, aged 43, to an attractive Birmingham lass, Rita Painting, and they had bought a house and settled near Solihull, in the south of greater Birmingham. Rita came from a musical family with her mother, for example, having sung at Digbeth Institute, in Birmingham; and Rita herself was an excellent pianist, so much so that Jack considered having her in his band at one time. Jack was also a fair singer and he would serenade Rita if she came to any of his dances by singing the old Irish favourite: 'Rose of Tralee'. Like most of us Dales, he was a born romantic!

Perhaps with reluctance, he decided to go back to a regular working life and applied for, and got a position at the Rover Car Company in the stores department. His engineering background probably helped a little in this situation. He did not abandon music but concentrated on providing customised bands for all occasions. Weddings, company dances, Masonic dances and dinner dances were some examples of the range of events, and the size of the band varied depending on the organiser's budget, and the importance of the occasion. This work was mainly in the evenings and the weekends, and he continued into the 1970s providing this tailor-made service. In due course he put aside his saxophone and clarinet and enjoyed his retirement. Golf, gardening and following Aston Villa were three of his interests.

I liked my Uncle Jack a lot. He had a great sense of humour and enjoyed a good story or a joke. I think he worked hard during his dance band days but he also played hard as well, with golf his main interest. My dad and both his brothers graced the golf courses of Britain and often played each other when they met up. The Dale competitive streak came to the fore but there was no rancour; they all remained the best of friends regardless of who won. Uncle Jack did amuse me when he claimed once he had never lost his Edinburgh accent in spite of living in Birmingham for some 60 years. To my Scottish ears, he spoke in distinctive 'Brummy' but I never had the courage to tell him!

Jack did admit in his memoirs that being a 'little bloke' he would stick up for himself. He said it was like 'a suit of armour; some people would call it stubbornness and possibly arrogance', but he felt if he was right, he would not be shifted. There were examples in his life, one or two in the public domain, where this trait emerged. For example, when he moved to Birmingham in the 1920s he was recruited at £6 per week for six months to play the saxophone with Al Roach and his band, an outfit that played at Tony's Ballroom in Hurst Street. But with the Depression, the ballroom management asked Roach to reduce the band from seven members to five and Jack was fired after three months. Jack took Roach to court asking for the balance of his contract money. The judge expressed sympathy for the music industry at this time, but agreed that there was no evidence the management were dissatisfied with Jack's playing and indeed he had been appointed deputy conductor of the band. He won his case with an award of nine weeks salary, less £1 which he had been paid for one night's work, giving him a net figure of £53.

I detected features of his grandfather, Henry Thomas Dale, and his father, Harry Wamba Dale, in his character and there was no disgrace in that as all of them were quite successful in their own way. Determination, professionalism, honesty and creativity were their strengths, accompanied by humour, and respect for their patrons as well as their colleagues. In my opinion, that made a fine cocktail of attributes.

Much to my surprise, he never travelled outside Britain, preferring to holiday in the south-west – Cornwall, Devon and Dorset – with forays to Wales and his favourite seaside resort, Scarborough. The longevity of the Dale genes gave him a good run and he died on 24 August 1991, aged 88, in Birmingham. He left behind a lot of nice memories and much in the way of press cuttings, photographs and other memorabilia. Sadly, there were no children from his marriage so that particular Dale line has ceased but his abilities are still remembered in publications about Birmingham and the great days of the dance halls.

Jack Dale on the right with clarinet rehearsing in Scarborough in 1949
(Dale Collection)

THE DALE DIASPORA

T he word 'diaspora' is well accepted in modern language and is to be found with increasing regularity in the press and other media. The dictionary definition is 'a dispersion', from the Greek 'dia' meaning through, and 'speirein' meaning a scattering. Originally applied to the Jews after the Babylonian captivity, it is now applied, almost as a cliché, to the Irish after the famine of the 1840s, and the Scots after the Highland clearances from about 1820 to the 1890s. The Scots, for example, 'dispersed', from their native land to the USA, Canada, Australia, New Zealand, South Africa and elsewhere to find work and a future for their families. Many recognisable Scottish surnames are now found commonly in these countries providing a genealogical clue to those looking for their roots.

This little family history of my Dale ancestors is no exception to the diaspora phenomenon, as I am aware of relatives, some quite distant but still sporting the four letter surname, who can currently be found in the USA, Canada and Australia. Within the United Kingdom itself, the branch of the family I have been concerned with had its origins in the midlands of England around Staffordshire and Warwickshire, but is now dispersed throughout the land in Cheshire, Cornwall, Gloucestershire, the Isle of Man, the Isle of Wight, Lancashire, Lincolnshire, Northumberland, Yorkshire, and in Scotland can be found in both Edinburgh and Glasgow.

Fortunately, modern communications has enabled these distant scions to keep in touch which contrasts with the 19th-century scattering of the Irish and the Scots, where, once they had departed from their native country, ongoing contact was minimal, if not impossible. As our planet shrinks in size, no doubt the Dales will explore other remote corners and continue their colonisation of the earth, if not beyond!

The National Trust has an informative website where distribution maps of specific surnames in Britain have been constructed. Two dates have been used to illustrate the spread of these names, in 1881 and 1998. Examining the 1881 map for the surname 'Dale' reveals that the largest concentration of people bearing that surname lived in the Midlands around Warwickshire and Staffordshire, Yorkshire, parts of East Anglia and a pocket in Cornwall. There are hardly any Dales in Wales, while the only prominent Scottish area was Ayrshire and the Isle of Arran in the west of the country.

By 1998, 117 years later, the distribution of the name had expanded mainly in the east of England up to Northumberland, and south to Kent. There was a slight reduction in the east midlands but the west midlands had grown. Cornwall remained an isolated pocket and Wales still lacked any real presence while Scotland's share had hardly changed. In London, from being found in the north, east, west and south of the capital in 1881, the concentration in 1998 is predominantly in the south of the metropolis. All very interesting and slightly relevant to my specific family branch as some of these nomads undoubtedly had their ancestral origins in my branch of the family. So the family name distribution has expanded, and will probably continue to do so in the next 100 years.

But do our roots really matter? Is there a need to seek out our origins and trace descent from an early ancestor? History, in all its forms, is of interest to many people and I subscribe to the theory that we can all learn from the past, and the present can influence the future. How our ancestors behaved affected their children, just as my children have been moulded by the attitudes and behaviour of their parents. You can be shocked, proud, amazed, concerned, amused, sad, annoyed, or respectful towards your ancestors but inherently, they have planted some aspects of themselves within you. Every family has its secrets, good and bad, so finding the origin of these can be fulfilling, as well as interesting.

I am always impressed how the ordinary Victorians, for example, survived and prospered whilst surrounded by poverty, disease and malnutrition. The story of ordinary folk, their lifestyle, survival and expansion can be more relevant in social terms than that of the aristocracy. The ordinary folk were the power house of this country, the hands-on doers who created wealth for the better-off. It is much more difficult to trace their story, but, for the same reason, much more satisfying when results about them emerge from the mists of time.

I have tried to give a good solid background to three generations of the Dales starting with Henry Thomas Dale. The fourth generation, of which I am a member, and their descendants will carry aspects of the Dale genes no matter how diluted. I have been impressed by the musical gene, for example, which was strong for three generations of my branch, and I am aware of fourth and fifth generation members of the same branch who have similar skills and perform publicly in, for example, brass bands and modern music groups. On a personal level, I have no instrumental talents, but I had a good singing voice when younger performing in school and church choirs. My one and only appearance in front of a theatre audience was in the annual school play back in the late 1950s when I was cast as Gratiano, the playboy, in *The Merchant of Venice*. Some would say I was typecast, but I did achieve a mention in the *Edinburgh Evening News* where I was described as a 'relaxed Gratiano'. It is always best to retire when you are at your peak, so I stepped down from the stage and concentrated on sport and girls thereafter!

Humour is another genetic feature of my ancestors, and there is no doubt that the many members I have met over the years have inherited that as well. Longevity has been mixed, with a number of males and females surviving into their late eighties and early nineties but others struggling to get to three score years and ten – other factors such as environment, diet and lifestyle have perhaps influenced their early departure. An interesting observation, totally subjective in character, has been the facial features of many of my extended family members. From family photographs of distantly related Dales, there are similarities such that when I got off a train on a crowded station platform to meet a second cousin for the very first time, I instantly recognised him as his appearance reminded me immediately of my father's oldest brother. The joy of family history research is to have all these occasions happen, and immediately have a common bond with someone who was previously a complete stranger.

But there are also dangers. Not every family member wants to know his or her origins in fine detail as there might be situations that he or she had been unaware of, or had successfully hidden for years that might now be revealed. I have come across a couple of these problems in my research that do not appear in this book. As a result, I made a promise to the people concerned that I would not embarrass them by talking about their part in the family history, and I have honoured that promise. Without gaining their confidence in this way, I would have had gaps in my knowledge, and not gained access to a number of photographs and other memorabilia.

The factual information about a family and its origins can readily be assembled from the birth, marriage and death certificates and census data, provided by the Register Offices in England, Scotland and elsewhere. However, these facts are only the skeleton and there is much flesh that needs to be hung on the bones. Interviewing older relatives is useful, even if they make mistakes in dates, names, relationships and so on, while accessing photographs, letters, press cuttings and other written material can supplement existing knowledge. I think it is fair to say that once a family history is launched, there is unlikely to be an end – ever! There are always holes in the data, mysterious situations, unexplained happenings, lost individuals, unrecorded facts and of course, deliberate obfuscation that never allows a researcher to complete the jigsaw. I have read of some researchers who are still seeking answers after twenty years and they may never get that final clue which will provide the last piece in the jigsaw. I have been conducting my own research over a nine-year period and I still seek many answers! But, glory halleluia, when something new does fall into place and another mystery is solved, for then there is a great deal of satisfaction to follow.

I have enjoyed, like so many other TV viewers, the various episodes of the BBC series: *Who Do You Think You Are* but there is something wrong when a life story is presented in a one-hour slot and the impression given is that all the facts were readily available. I suspect, in reality, a team of professional researchers laboured away for months gathering the data at some expense, and even then the presentation may have been edited if insufficient material was available. I am a true amateur researcher and have never considered engaging professional researchers except when geography and time were against me. I have enjoyed carrying out my own research and travelling to the Midlands, Cheshire and Lancashire, for example, seeking out where my ancestors lived and relating the places in which they were domiciled to their personal circumstances. I have also found that Family History Societies and local libraries throughout the country have bent over backwards to help me, and I thank those largely unsung heroes most sincerely.

I have often asked myself if the story of my family was worth telling. As I draw to the end of this process, the answer is obviously 'yes', but I have been fortunate in having ancestors who followed an unusual path, entering the entertainment business when it was still developing and achieving some modest success. Perhaps if the various generations had been agricultural labourers or miners, and never deviated from these honest and worthy occupations, the story might have been less interesting to the outsider. The aristocracy of this country can often trace their ancestry back many generations as all personal matters were carefully recorded within their family since inheritance in terms of title and wealth were important to them. To ordinary families – and I include my own in that definition – the past seemed less important as there was little wealth or property to pass on, and there were no titles. Yet the story is no less interesting when a humble file cutter born into a dirty, industrial environment dragged himself out of his hard and sweaty existence, to carve a career where his performances were appreciated and measured by the audience reaction. Sir Harry Lauder, the great Scots comedian, is reputed to have said he did not give his audiences any more entertainment than was necessary, but left them with their mouths watering for more. No entertainer has the right to expect his audience to welcome him, or her, without question, but a genuine artist will survive criticism, learn from it, and perhaps improve because of it. Henry Thomas Dale served two apprenticeships, the first as a file cutter, the second, more extensively, as a performer in front of a live audience. I also think he never stopped learning right up to the day he retired from the business, as tastes changed, patrons demanded more, managers demanded more, new generations sought other angles on familiar themes, and the pace of the performances would also change.

My admiration for him during his entertainment days encompasses the ability to produce 11 children, 10 of whom survived, whom he somehow or other gave an adequate education, nearly all of whom he taught at least one instrument, and to read music. He also made sure that those who chose an entertainment career were suitably launched on an acceptable path. His wife, Sarah Ann, needs to be given much credit as well for keeping the family together, producing and raising so many lusty children, raising money from her own activities when required, and being extremely supportive. For a lady known to be less than five feet in height, she had amazing energy. She was loved and revered by her offspring all her long life.

The career of Henry Thomas also needs to be put into context. When he started in the business the Victorian era was comparatively young, the horse was vitally important, and the steam and the railway system was just developing but when he retired in 1909, many marvellous things had happened. The railway network had spread across the country, the petrol and diesel engine had revolutionised personal transport, the ability to fly was in its early days, electricity was available for power and light, the film industry had been born, and Marconi had demonstrated how radio waves could open up the world by improving communications. It is also worth mentioning that he lived within the reigns of three sovereigns, Victoria, Edward VII and George V.

My grandfather, Harry Wamba Dale, lived within the reigns of six sovereigns from Victoria to Elizabeth II, and witnessed three major wars. Technology advanced at a rapid pace with the telephone, radio, TV, film and recording industries influencing the entertainment business, whilst medical advances ensured a decline in infant mortality, and both men and women lived longer. In my father's case, he was enchanted by colour television, saw travel around the world made almost routine, and lived long enough to see man stand on the moon, yet he died only 135 years after his grandfather, Henry Thomas, was born.

Looking briefly at the names of the 10 surviving children of Harry and Sarah Ann Dale, and examining subsequent generations, it can be seen that several Christian names are repeated within the family, even up to the present day. Naming patterns are quite common in most countries and one of the most familiar patterns was the eldest son being named after the paternal grandfather, the second son named after the maternal grandfather, the third son named after the father. The eldest daughter was named after the maternal grandmother, the second daughter named after the paternal grandmother and the third daughter named after the mother. These patterns can be quite helpful if a researcher is faced with several options when seeking an ancestor. Within the male side of my branch of the Dale family, the most common name is Harry, the diminutive of Henry, where the earliest I have found is dated about 1820 and the latest 2010. Stanley, Albert and John are persistent with, to a lesser extent, Sydney, Ernest, Alan and William. It is only when my generation is reached that less traditional names start to appear. On the female side, the most used name, but not necessarily the prime Christian name, is Mercia, and with less frequency other names found include Vera, Dorothy and Lottie/Charlotte.

Moving on beyond Henry Thomas Dale, of the boys in his family, Harry and Albert were the disciples of their father in the early days and when their act split up, each in his own way did well although the world around them then changed their future quite dramatically. The First World War caused significant upheaval in the social engineering within this country, and it was never the same again. The loss of so many young men was a catastrophe, but it allowed thousands of women to show they were as talented in the work place as they were in the home. The pre-war ways of men and women changed and Harry and Albert had to adapt to the change around them. Sydney Edgar continued in the music business but, with three marriages, the strains on his private life showed. Ernest, although not a professional entertainer, was influenced by the First World War as he married a young war widow after the loss of his first wife, and suddenly had a family in his forties. Stanley, of course, was a victim of the war as was Ella's husband, Gus Coyne. The girls, with the exception of Amy who died in 1905, got on with their lives as mothers and home-makers after the war, although there did seem to be a hidden problem as three of them had early deaths – Amy, Lottie in 1924, and Vera Maud in 1937. The other two daughters, Ella and Doris May, lived on to 87 and 93 respectively.

The next generation produced fewer children and the generation after that fewer still. As the standard of living rose, the number of children born reduced as there was less infant mortality and families entered the era of 'planned' parenthood, abandoning the Victorian habit of a child every two years until the mother either died from exhaustion or a birth-related illness. The result of this is that there are fewer Dale members to spread across the earth but the ones that are around tend to be healthier, so I am hopeful my family name will continue for many generations to come.

I would recommend anyone who is interested to take a

genealogical journey. 'Tinker, tailor, soldier, sailor, rich man, poor man, beggar man, thief' as the child's rhyme has it, probably includes at least someone who exists in every family tree. As I have indicated above, it will take time and attributes such as patience, logic, persistence, and an ability to organise results will be essential. The results will never be wasted, whether it is the spear side, i.e. male line, or the distaff side, i.e. female line.

On page 3 I revealed that I started my research with a blank sheet of paper. Some nine years later I have accumulated a large archive of material: documents – official and unofficial – books, photographs and other memorabilia that occupy a lot of shelf space. Covering almost 200 years in my investigations I have noted the many changes in society that have taken place and the affect – good and bad – on my ancestors. This voyage of discovery has been a positive feature for me as I have learnt new things about myself and that must be a good thing.

BIBLIOGRAPHY

REFERENCES

British Theatre & Music Halls by John Earl, Shire Publications,
   Princess Risborough, 2005
Miss Cranston's Omnibus by Anna Blair, Lomond Books,
   Edinburgh, 1998
Popular Entertainments through the Ages by Samuel McKechnie.
   Sampson Low, Marston & Co., London, 1930s?
Scotland & the Music Hall 1850–1914 by Paul Maloney, Manchester
   University Press, Manchester. 2003
Scottish Showbusiness, Music Hall, Variety & Pantomime by Frank
   Bruce, NMS Publishing, Edinburgh, 2000
The Story of the Britannia Music Hall by Judith Bowers, Birlinn,
   Edinburgh, 2007
Victorian Arena, The Performers. Volume 1 by John Turner,
   Lingdales Press, Formby. 1995
Victorian Arena, The Performers, Volume 2 by John Turner,
   Lingdales Press, Formby, 2000

SOURCES

Unpublished document by Bert Dale, 1979
Unpublished document by Jack Dale, 1981
The Era, weekly newspaper. Internet
The Stage, weekly newspaper, Internet.
Reports in the *Edinburgh Evening News, Glasgow Herald, The
   Scotsman, Warrington Guardian, Birmingham Post, Radio
   Times, World's Fair*
Aberdeen Public Library
Birmingham Central Library
Bodleian Library, Oxford University
Carlisle Public Library

Commonwealth War Graves Commission, London
Dundee Public Library
Edinburgh Room, Central Library, Edinburgh
General Register Office, Southport
General Register Office Scotland, Edinburgh
Hartlepool Public Library
Manchester & Lancashire FHS, Manchester
Mitchell Library, Glasgow
National Archives, Kew, London
National Archives Scotland, Edinburgh
National Library, London.
National Library Scotland, Edinburgh
Newcastle Public Library
Oldham Public Library
Powys Family History Society
Scottish Genealogy Society, Edinburgh
Walsall Public Library
Wellington Aviation Museum, Moreton-in-Marsh
Wolverhampton Public Library

INDEX

Page numbers in bold italics refer to illustrations.